TYING FLIES
For Trophy Trout

with
Jack Shaw

Illustrations by John Moutray

HERITAGE HOUSE

Copyright © 1992, 1999 Jack Shaw

CANADIAN CATALOGUING IN PUBLICATION DATA

Shaw, Jack, 1916-
   Tying flies for trophy trout

   ISBN 1-895811-37-6

   1. Trout fishing. 2. Fly tying. 3. Fly fishing.. I. Title.
SH687.S53 1999   799.1'757   C99-910340-7

First edition - 1992
First Heritage House edition - 1999

All rights reserved. No part of this publication may be reproduced, stored in a retrieval system, or transmitted in any form or by any means—electronic, mechanical, photocopying, audio recording, or otherwise—without the written permission of the publisher or, in the case of photocopying, a licence from CANCOPY, Toronto, Canada.

Heritage House wishes to acknowledge the Book Publishing Industry Development Program of Heritage Canada, the British Columbia Arts Council, and the Canada Council for the Arts for supporting various aspects of our publishing program.

Photography by Jack Shaw
Design and layout by Darlene Nickull
Edited by Ron Nelson, Audrey McClellan

HERITAGE HOUSE PUBLISHING COMPANY LTD.
Unit #8 - 17921 55th Ave., Surrey, BC V3S 6C4

Printed in Canada

Dedication

To all fly fishers concerned enough to keep our environment clean.

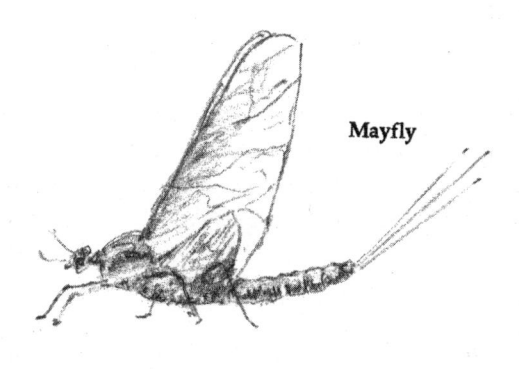

Mayfly

Acknowledgements

My thanks and sincere appreciation to my wife, Dorothy, for reading and rereading, making the many corrections necessary, and for all her words of encouragement; and to Ron Boudreau for his talented assistance with some of the photography

Contents

In Appreciation—by Mike Cramond	7
Introduction	9
PART ONE: FUNDAMENTALS OF FLY TYING	11
Chapter 1—The Art of Fly Tying	12
Chapter 2—Hackle: Hair, Fur, and Feathers	15
Chapter 3—Other Fly-Tying Materials	20
Chapter 4—Fly Hooks	24
Chapter 5—Tools and Fly-Tying Aids	29
Tinsel-Making Machine	35
The CO_2 Cartridge Bobbin	36
Carding Brushes	41
Velcro Brush	42
Setting Fur and Feathers	42
Rejuvenating Flies and Feathers	44
Curling Feathers and Fur	44
Dyeing Your Own Material	44
Bleaching Natural Materials	46
Chapter 6—Dubbing	47

Chapter 7—Problems of a Novice Fly Tyer	50
Placing the Hook in the Vise	50
Starting the Thread on the Hook	50
Making the Tail	52
Making the Body	53
Tying on Wings	53
Keeping the Right Bobbin Tension	55
Using the Whipfinisher	55
Finishing the Head Without a Whipfinishing Tool	59
Half Hitch With a Pen	60
PART TWO: THE POINT OF THE GAME	**62**
Chapter 8—Impression and Imitation	63
Chapter 9—A Detective Story	70
PART THREE: FLY TYING FOR EVERYONE	**74**
Chapter 10—Making the Flies	75
Woolly Worm (Sedgefly Larva)	75
Blood Worm	77
Leech	81
Terrestrial Traveller Sedgefly	84
Water Boatman	87
Mayfly Nymph	91

Mayfly Dun	94
Mayfly Spinner	96
Damselfly Nymph	98
Chironomid Pupa	102
Sedgefly Pupa	107
Emerging Chironomid	111
Shrimp	114
Dragonfly Nymph	118
Gomphus Dragonfly Nymph	124
Nation's Red Dragon	127

PART FOUR: A CLOSER LOOK AT CHIRONOMID FISHING — 145

Chapter 11—In The Beginning	146
Chapter 12—Chironomid Gear	149
Chapter 13—Altered Chironomid Flies	151
Black Chironomid with Gold Rib	151
Two Tone Chironomid	152
Half Pink Chironomid	153
Chapter 14—Thoughts in Closing	156

In Appreciation

By Mike Cramond

(Now retired, Mike Cramond was Outdoor Editor of the Vancouver Province *for 24 years. He is the author of nine outdoor books and winner of ten national and international awards for features on conservation.)*

Jack Shaw lives in Kamloops, surrounded by British Columbia's famous Kamloops trout country. He has spent a great many years raising insects the way many people raise goldfish. He then studies and photographs them throughout their life cycle so that he can simulate Nature's food chain. In addition, he has spent literally years on lakes from ice-out to freeze-up, observing insects and trout in their natural element.

If you have ever been lucky enough to have one of Jack's flies on your tippet, you were in possession of an excellent advantage over the trout you seek. His flies are a revelation in duplication of freshwater insect life, based on his years of study in his basement laboratory and in the field. If you were fortunate enough to watch Jack fish that fly, or any other, you were probably out-fished that day. Jack, in my opinion, knows more about how to fly fish successfully in trout lakes than anyone else in the world. He regularly comes away with a string when everyone else on the lake has been skunked.

This expertise resulted in Jack introducing a radical concept to B.C. fly fishing—using flies with no wings. Veteran B.C. author/angler Bob Jones described this break with tradition in a profile on Jack in *BC Outdoors* magazine:

> In 1966, while employed at a body shop, Jack developed an allergic skin reaction to the dust. He left to take work as a sales clerk and fly tyer at Burfield's Ski and Sport Shop. When his boss suggested he tie some of his own patterns for sale, Jack produced a series of chironomids he had developed in 1962. They didn't sell.

"People weren't used to flies without wings," he recalled. "I had to actually start giving fishing lessons on how to fish a chironomid in order to sell them. It became a damned nuisance, but in the process a lot of fellows were educated on how to become chironomid fishermen."

Over the years, Jack has developed several popular patterns. "I started tying the Blood Leech and Blood Worm about 1965. There were the Damselfly Nymph and the Dragonfly Nymph, which became known as the Jules Nymph. The McLean's Special was originally my Brown Sedge. When I first introduced them I had quite a time selling them. Nymph fishing was unknown around here at that time and the fishermen were reluctant to try something new. The big flies then were Nation's Fancy and so on. Like I said, I was fighting tradition by trying to educate people to fish flies that didn't have wings. Some guys got right argumentative.

"It was a long struggle, but it eventually caught on."

Jack Shaw is my friend, and I know him not only as a superb angler but also as a dedicated conservationist. The latter aspect of his life was recognized in 1990 when the Stave Lake Correctional Centre named its trout farm the Jack Shaw Trout Enhancement Project. The facility annually raises thousands of trout, which are then used for stocking lakes.

At the dedication ceremony, Local Director L. Boon noted: "I am particularly pleased that we are now able to recognize the outstanding achievements and contribution of a B.C. citizen to the sport of fishing. I am hopeful that our efforts will equal your well-deserved reputation."

This book is Jack's second. His first, *Fly Fish the Trout Lakes*, appeared in 1976 and was reprinted several times. It was updated in 1998 and remains a popular bestseller.

I have long awaited this new book of Jack's extremely pertinent knowledge. As a fellow angler, with him many times in the field, I hope it will help the rest of us understand why he so consistently out-fishes us—regardless of the hatch hovering in the air or on the water.

Introduction

Fly fishing is a sport that has been practised for several thousand years. The earliest popular writing on the sport is credited to Izaak Walton (1593-1683), an English author and angler who published *The Compleat Angler* in 1653. After more than 300 years, his book is still regarded as the masterwork for the angling fraternity.

In early times only kings, lords, and gentry partook in the sport of fishing. The difference today is that we common folk have joined the elite.

British and European gentry immigrating to the New World recognized the potential for some fine sport and quickly took advantage of it. Fly fishing rapidly spread westward across the American and Canadian wilds. At first it was practised mainly on rivers and streams, but it expanded to many small lakes as they were stocked with fish to challenge the angler.

One species that has been used to stock lakes and streams all over the world, from New Zealand to Argentina, is B.C.'s famous Kamloops trout. The alkaline quality of the water in and around Kamloops itself is an ideal environment for this celebrated species and the many organisms on which it feeds. The region's elevation and seasonal temperature variations create the ideal water temperature for growing strong fish of exceptional fighting quality.

As noted later in this book, the fly fisherman has at all times to consider the environment in which fish are found. Because weather, water quality, vegetation, temperature, and moon phases have a strong effect on trout feeding, it follows that the successful angler must always keep these factors in mind when fishing and dressing flies.

I find that I gain the most from fly fishing by dressing my own flies. It's an absorbing but relaxing activity, and the satisfaction I feel when I catch a fish on a fly of my own creation is a joy that has to be experienced to be appreciated. Doing your own fly tying is often the only way a realistic pattern can be obtained. Commercial patterns that are consistent in size, colour, material, and quality are hard to find.

Compared to other popular activities such as skiing or photography, fly-tying costs are modest—less than $200 for equipment, while an additional $100 provides enough fly-dressing materials to last several seasons. A person does not have to be nimble-fingered to dress flies—an advantage for those with arthritis—as there are tools available that eliminate the need for dexterity but none of the pleasure.

In order to tie flies with accuracy and intelligence, it is imperative that you acquire a reasonable knowledge of an insect's appearance. My earlier book, *Fly Fish the Trout Lakes*, has many photographs of the insects on which trout feed. There is also a detailed life profile of each individual insect as it pertains to fly fishing.

In this book, the chapter on fly patterns is not arranged in order of biological development. Instead, the flies are described in order of difficulty to dress. If the flies are tied in the order given, when all are completed the most useful techniques will have been used. The reader will be well on the way to becoming a proficient fly tyer.

It is the dream of most fly fishermen to catch a trophy trout—a fish over four pounds, or about two kilograms. The hopeful angler spends many hours searching for materials and devising combinations of material and technique that may entice the uncommonly large trout to do battle. He then hopes for the emotional control and manual dexterity that will bring such a worthy adversary to the net. And, always, he respects the wonderful abilities of the trout he seeks. In their natural environment, they are as smart as we are in ours.

There is an old saying that Allah does not take from one's allotted life span the days spent fishing. I don't know if Allah keeps a record, but I often wonder if Izaak Walton's long life was the result of his practising this activity. In the days when the average life span was about 40 years, he lived to be 90, the equivalent of over two lifetimes.

Good fishing.
Jack Shaw
Kamloops, B.C.

PART ONE

FUNDAMENTALS OF FLY TYING

Chapter 1

The Art of Fly Tying

The mechanics of fly tying are not difficult to master. Creating a pattern to imitate an insect is, however, far more challenging and involved, requiring considerable imagination and artistic ability. As in many art forms, what appears easy soon reveals itself to be far more complex than simply putting material on a hook.

The materials we use have characteristics ranging from colour, markings, and texture to the way they absorb or transmit light. Some materials absorb water in varying degrees, a characteristic that can change their colour and must be taken into account when dressing a fly pattern. Other materials that do not absorb water are more buoyant, a useful characteristic when dressing dry flies.

Before starting to dress a fly, we must obviously consider just what materials will best represent the food item we hope to imitate. Every little detail is important.

Style and size of the hook should be the first decision. For a dry fly, select a fine wire hook, preferably forged. For a wet fly, the weight of the hook is not often a factor, so standard weight hooks are suitable. On some patterns we may want to use especially heavy wire hooks. Streamer flies usually require a long-shank hook to accommodate the long body. Colour will depend on many things, including the water, the season, the insect's stage of growth (they are usually much paler as early instars, the early stage of development), the immediate environment, and the insect's or other invertebrate's food (which affects body colour).

To create the impression of an insect's movement, such as leg and body contractions and expansions, we must select material of suitable texture. The hackle feathers for a dry fly, for instance, should be what is called "hard," or stiff, to permit a lighter, more natural dressing and to provide adequate support on the water's surface. For the wet fly, a softer hackle feather should generally be used. Soft hackle moves more readily in the water and gives a good imitation of the legs used for swimming.

Fur dubbing on the body is inclined to contract and expand when retrieved through the water, imparting a very lifelike movement. In addition, light passing through the outer fuzzy fibres gives the body a natural translucent appearance. On some insect imitations, certain areas of the dubbing can be left long to represent legs. If the texture is right, the imitation will move with great authenticity. Because soft material may mat if it is too long, careful selection is important and results in fuller creels.

I find that tinsel use is in many cases overdone, creating attractor-type flies rather than imitations. When used correctly, however, tinsel is vital. Many invertebrate trout foods—shrimp, beetle larvae, some dragonfly nymphs, and some insects in the pupal stages—have an exceptionally hard exoskeleton, or external structure. This exoskeleton is usually segmented and curves to the joints between segments. Under some conditions, this curve reflects light off certain portions. Here tinsel, wisely applied, greatly adds to the natural appearance.

Another seldom-considered use for tinsel is very important. During the process called "photosynthesis," plants give off tiny bubbles of oxygen. Insects that move among the weeds gather these bubbles in the angles of legs, in body segments, and in hair. Like tiny silver balls, the bubbles reflect light. You can use tinsel to represent this condition extremely effectively.

In autumn the quality of light changes considerably. At this season, dark-water lakes are best fished with flies that are dressed with gold tinsel rather than silver.

Many fly tyers become so involved in the study of aquatic insects that they lose sight of their original purpose. They try to place each specimen in the proper niche of order, species, and genus, etc. This process is complicated, involved, and not in the least necessary since the divisions, in many cases, require microscopic examination. As anglers, we should be concerned only with the normally visible characteristics usually sufficient to place invertebrates into their correct order, sub-order, and family. If an angler is sufficiently knowledgeable to identify a terrestrial and its nymph or pupal form along with size, colour, and movement, other information that more closely identifies the insect is not important. Charting the veining in the caudal appendages and gills, measuring the length of the tibia, and other microscopic features are best left to the biologist.

Remember that we cannot create an insect. We must therefore strive to create the impression of one through size, colour, movement, or whatever other means we can devise.

Chapter 2

Hackle: Hair, Fur, and Feathers

To the average fly fisher the term "hackle feathers" means the feathers on a rooster's neck. This assumption is true to a degree, but other feathers are also called hackle. To add to confusion, many kinds of animal hair and artificial materials are called hackle when they are used for fly tying. In fact, almost any material used to represent legs on a fly pattern can correctly be called hackle. The feathers on a bird's neck and the hair that stands up and bristles on a dog, moose, bear, or many other animals when they are challenged, also are called hackle.

Among the fly-tying fraternity, **feathers** from a wide range of birds are used for hackles. They are selected for such characteristics as their hardness or softness, length, colour, and markings known as "modelling." A single bird can provide varied types of hackle feathers. Notable among these birds are the various pheasants, particularly the males.

Most good fly-tying supply houses carry a wide selection of feathers, some still attached to the skin, others loose packaged. Rooster-neck feathers are best bought as a cape. While this may at first appear to be expensive, it isn't. The main benefit is that you will be able to select the right size without searching through a bag of loose feathers with the prospect of a fight with static electricity, which you usually lose. One or two such experiences quickly make it apparent which is the best buy.

Rooster-neck hackle is used almost exclusively on dry-fly patterns. It must be taken from a mature bird in order to be stiff, hard, and of good enough quality to properly support the fly on the water.

Wet-fly patterns can, and do, make use of softer feathers like hen-neck hackle and many types of body feathers. Being soft, they move more easily when drawn through the water, creating a realistic impression of a live insect.

Variegated colours, spots, and bars in any number of sizes, shapes, and shades are found on the body plumage of a great many birds. For this reason, if you have a knowledge of the characteristics of a number of feathers and their source, it is not difficult to find a feather that will exactly meet your requirements.

Wing quills—the flight feathers on wings—are divided into primary and secondary quills. The primary quills are also called "pointers." They are found on the first section of wing, from the tip to the first joint. The secondary quills are on the section from the first joint to the elbow, or second joint. The feathers on top of the wing from the leading edge back are known as "coverts." For dressing trout flies, however, we are interested only in the wing quills mentioned above. Other wing feathers are so little used they are of no great importance to fly tyers.

Wing quills are usually used for making wings on trout flies, so they should be used in pairs; that is, a quill from the right-hand wing should be used with the matching quill from the left-hand wing. The reason for this is the natural curve of these feathers. If a fly is dressed with wings made from a single feather, it will be inclined to spin when it is retrieved, the amount of spin depending on the speed at which it is retrieved.

Other characteristics of wing quills can also be important. The leading side of a wing quill (primary and secondary) is usually shorter and stiffer than the trailing side and curves only one way. By contrast, the trailing side frequently has a reverse curve, and its edge is not always smooth and well defined. On many of the larger birds, the ragged edges of the trailing side often create a problem and must be trimmed by singeing or cutting. To do this, I make allowance for what has to be removed when I tie the wings on. Then, holding them between two dimes in the proper position, I burn the ragged edges with a punk stick or a cigarette and brush them lightly with fine sandpaper. The alternative is to trim with a pair of sharp scissors before or after removal from the quill. Take off as little as possible, and be careful lest the feather be ruined.

Feather flues (the fibres on each side of the feather's stem) are also used as fly-body materials. They vary greatly in colour, markings, and texture. Some species of owl, for example, have a soft velvety flue that is very furry. While it is useful, it is

Hackle: Hair, Fur, and Feathers 17

unfortunately soft and not terribly durable. Peacock and emu fibres (also known as herl) are especially popular, but almost any flue can be wound onto a hook shank to create a distinctive body. The flues from ring-neck pheasant tail feathers are the basis for several very effective patterns.

The fur and hair of many animals are used in fly dressing. Many people don't realize that animals have both fur and hair. **Fur** is the part of a pelt (animal skin) that insulates the animal's body from the elements. It is extremely fine, soft, and usually grows quite thick. Hair—called **guard hair**—grows through the fur. It is not nearly as dense, is much coarser, and is a great deal longer.

Fur, minus the guard hair, is used to dress the bodies of many fly patterns. When it is spun on a thread and wound onto a hook it is called "dubbing." Fur of different colours, natural and dyed, can be mixed together to achieve a variety of colours and shades. Dubbing has an advantage over many fly-body materials since it can be made to whatever dimension is required and is light and durable. Most importantly, it imparts a lifelike appearance owing to the translucence and gentle movement of the outer surface.

Hair is also used for trout fly dressings—usually for wings and tails but also for "spun" bodies. Some of the more useful large animals are deer, moose, bear, caribou, elk, mountain goat, and mountain sheep; of the smaller animals, squirrel, badger, marmot, beaver, and muskrat are used.

Deer hair, particularly from the white-tail, is the most popular. All deer hair is hollow and therefore lightweight. White-tail hair, however, is softer and tougher than mule deer hair, and the ends are much more even. In winter, white-tail hair ranges from dark to light grey, with that of its large tail—sometimes called the "flag"—mostly white. Belly hair is of similar colour. In summer, body hair is quite different in colour, ranging from medium yellowish tan to a rich golden tan. The latter is a useful colour but hard to find. In winter the body hair is about 2 inches (5 centimetres) long; in summer it is about half that length.

Mule deer hair is similar to that of the white-tail but is coarser, and the ends are not as even or as tough. Because it is harder, it does not stand up as well in use. This criticism does not mean that it is of no value. It is a very good and useful hair, and if it is properly treated on the hide is only of slightly less quality than that of the white-tail.

Moose hair is coarse, hard, and difficult to work with. Body hair is about 2 to 3 inches (5 to 8 centimetres) long and ranges in colour from dark sepia to black. The bull's mane is long and wiry, up to about 8 inches (20 centimetres) long, and is often a mixture of white, grey, brown, and black. The lighter-coloured hair takes dye readily and is long enough to make beautiful braided-body nymphs. It is also an excellent hair for making tails on many fly patterns.

Bear hair is much used in dressing many fly patterns. Polar bear hair is by far the most popular. It has a beautiful translucence that is most attractive to fish. The under-hair, too coarse to be called fur, is an excellent substitute for seal fur, which is no longer available. Polar bear hair is unsurpassed for wings on many steelhead and salmon flies. It is also used on a number of trout fly patterns.

Black bear hair is approximately 2 to 3 inches (5 to 8 centimetres) long and ranges from black through all shades of brown. The long, abundant guard hair is primarily used for wings and tails. The finer under-hair is quite crinkly and fairly short, about an inch (26 millimetres) long. Despite the bear's name, it is rare to find this hair in a true jet black; usually it is a rich sepia brown or dark tan. It is useful for some dubbing applications and also for the hackle on some flies.

Caribou, elk, and mountain sheep hair is quite similar to that of deer except for colour. These hairs, like those of deer, are hollow and most suitable for dressing dry flies. Colour is widely varied through tan, brown, and grey. The colours are often mixed and referred to as "roan," best described as a "salt and pepper" appearance.

The long guard hair from mountain goats is often called "the poor man's polar bear hair," but I feel that comparison is unworthy. There is not even a remote similarity, unless length of some of the hair is considered. Mountain goat hair lacks the translucence, texture, sheen, and durability of polar bear hair. Goat hair is a flat opaque white, and the tips are inclined to be brittle and frequently found broken off. It is most popular for dressing streamer fly patterns since it takes dye readily. In areas where large trout feed on various minnow species it is a popular material since the preferable polar bear hair is expensive and often difficult to find, particularly in extreme lengths. The goat's under-hair is rather coarse, much like that of the bear family. In over 30 years of tying flies I have never found a practical use for it.

Hackle: Hair, Fur, and Feathers   19

Squirrel tails are used extensively for the wings of many streamer fly patterns. Red, grey, black, and fox squirrel tails are all sold in the better fly-tying supply houses.

Badger hair is used for the wings of streamer flies and for unusual hackle effects. A long, fine-textured hair, it can be used on most average-size fly hooks with no undue stiffening of the wing. It is cream to buff coloured, with a dark grey or nearly black band becoming grizzly grey to near white as the colour lightens towards the tip of the hair. It is about 2 inches (5 centimetres) long. The under-fur makes a wonderful greyish buff dubbing that has many uses.

Beaver and muskrat guard hair makes high-quality hackle for many dry-fly patterns because it is tough and durable. Coming from animals whose natural element is water, the hair has a good texture that supports a fly well on the water without becoming soggy as many feathers do. Using guard hair as hackle may at first seem difficult. After a bit of practice, however, it becomes easy.

Calf tails, usually listed in catalogues as kip tails, are about 8 to 10 inches (20 to 25 centimetres) long. They are usually black and white, tan and white, or one solid colour, and are used for making wings on steelhead flies. Calf tails are often dyed, and fluorescent colours—hot orange, red, yellow, and green—are popular.

Many more kinds of fur and hair are useful and available from companies throughout the world. You can further add to your stock by investigating road kills or other animal mortalities. It is important that you take proper care of any finds. I have found that hair taken from a hide that was not salted immediately after removal from the animal and then properly tanned tends to be soft and easily cut by thread when it is being tied on a hook. While such untreated hides seem to have a reasonable following of enthusiastic users, I am not one of them. Possibly I have never been fortunate enough to acquire a good section of hide. I know many hides are nailed to a barn wall until dry, then given to fly-tying friends.

Chapter 3

Other Fly-Tying Materials

Webster's dictionary defines **tinsel** as "Thin sheets, strips, or threads of tin, metal foil, etc., used for inexpensive decoration." Ribbing is defined as "Ribs collectively; arrangement or collection of ribs, as in cloth, a ship, etc."

For fly tying, as mentioned above, tinsel is used to create the impression of body segments (ribs) natural to most insects. Originally tinsel for this purpose was made from strips of silver or "gold" (for obvious reasons the gold was made from brass rather than the genuine metal). In pre-plastic days, metal was used extensively, although it had a number of annoying characteristics. It would often tarnish badly, seriously impairing its usefulness. In addition, it was difficult to tie on without breaking and was very springy. As a consequence, on a stout body it was inclined to slip off.

Tinsel made of plastic Mylar is now most popular for fly dressing and is available in a number of styles, widths, shapes, and sizes. Plastic has many advantages over metal. It is available in a variety of colours and is lighter, which is particularly useful on dry flies and patterns that need to be as light as possible. Unlike metal, plastic tinsel does not tarnish and is less prone to kink and break when it is wrapped on a fly body, making it easier to use. About the only time metal is used today is for very fine wire types of ribbing material. In addition to tinsel, tape of various widths is used.

A design is embossed into some tinsel to create diamond-like facets that increase light-reflecting ability. Surprisingly, many of the embossed wire-like strands are made by spirally wrapping Mylar around a strand of thread. Called "oval gold" or "oval silver," you can buy this in small diameters.

Other Fly-Tying Materials 21

Lately, much of the tinsel has been made with gold on one side and silver on the other. I find this combination handy but hard to get used to since the colour facing you when it is tied on the hook determines the ribbing colour.

There are times when wide tinsel is required. If you need tinsel wider than what is commercially available, the solution is to buy an emergency survival blanket, or "space blanket" as it is usually called. These blankets, which are actually large sheets of plastic or Mylar, can be cut into strips as desired. Most sporting goods stores carry them in silver or gold.

Other ribbing material can be simple coloured thread in different diameters, copper wire, and copper tinsel. Although I have never seen copper tinsel commercially available, you can make your own by flattening a piece of wire. You can do this using an easily made machine that I describe on page 35.

Many fly tyers use only one **thread** for dressing all flies, usually black thread in 2/0, 4/0, or 6/0, made of cotton, silk, nylon, rayon, or one of the many synthetics on the market. The thread can be waxed or plain and is available in 50- and 200-yard (about 45- and 180-metre) spools. I prefer black, olive green, and a dark muddy brown thread, although occasionally cinnamon brown and insect green are useful. A 6/0 waxed cotton thread is strong enough to use on most flies but is still fine enough to keep bulk down on even the smallest patterns. Waxed rayon and a number of the new synthetic threads are excellent. They are consistent in size and quality, and even in the smallest sizes I haven't had an unreasonable amount of breakage. Silk thread is not readily available but that is not a problem as, compared with modern synthetics, it is not fine enough to be used for fly tying. Nylon thread is not suitable since it is stretchy, and in the 6/0 size it breaks a lot.

Wool for bodies can be from almost any knitting basket. For strands, however, finer wools are most easily handled. Tapestry wool is far superior to any others. It comes in small 15-yard (14-metre) hanks that are inexpensive. A tremendous variety of colours are available and this four-ply yarn can be easily split and used as a single strand. Thicker buffalo and Indian sweater wools are not suitable as the individual strands are too thick and cannot easily be divided. They therefore make lumpy, coarse bodies.

At times the imaginative fly tyer will find a specialty wool, usually in a wool shop, that looks appealing. Though such purchases often prove to be the equivalent of fool's gold, they occasionally turn into real treasure, compensating for the less useful material bought on speculation. When you find such a treasure, buy several balls because wool styles change rapidly and the colour could be discontinued. Keep in mind that the colour of wool changes considerably when wet—as a rule it becomes much darker. If colour shade is critical, saturate a snip in water so that you can accurately assess it.

An important point to remember when checking colour is to always use daylight or you will not get a true reading. Tungsten light casts an orange hue on the material, while fluorescent light usually imparts a greenish overtone. I have daylight colour-corrected lights over my tying bench so that colour tones are true. For those who own or have access to a Kelvin meter, suitable light has a colour temperature within a few degrees of 5500 degrees Kelvin. I use two 4-foot, daylight-corrected, fluorescent tubes. The maker is VITA-LITE and their specs are 40 watt, Duro-Test 33,000 hours, double cathode.

Commercial fly dressers who cannot afford the time to make dubbed bodies use a facsimile called "**chenille**." It is defined in Webster's dictionary as "A tufted velvety cord used for trimming embroidery, etc.," and is made of silk or rayon material laid at right angles between two strands of thread, then twisted tightly into a rope-like strand. Very popular, it is available in a wide range of sizes and colours. I, however, think bodies made from spun fur or hair are far superior.

Dubbing wax is applied to tying thread to aid adhesion of dubbed fur or hair. This mixture of several kinds of wax, fats, and resins is a slightly soft, rather sticky product usually sold in small cookie-like cakes. The ideal dubbing wax is not sticky on your hands, yet adheres well to the thread and dubbing material during the twisting operation. Once twisted, the strand can be picked out to whatever density is required and trimmed with a pair of scissors. Some base waxes for cross-country skis make good dubbing wax, but avoid any product that has a strong smell.

Most inexperienced fly tyers use too much dubbing (enough to dress four or five flies), then pick the excess off and discard it. Good dubbing material is too expensive to waste in that way.

Head cement is a type of lacquer that can be used on a hook over which the thread is wrapped. The cement prevents the body material from turning on the hook shank or being pulled down to the bend when taken by a fish. It is also applied to the butt of wings prior to the wraps, not only securing them but also gluing the hackle in place. After the head is tied off, head cement is also applied to the thread forming that head to further secure it and, to a degree, waterproof it.

For cement, I favour clear fingernail polish. It is sold in a small spill-proof bottle, has an applicator brush, and when it thickens from evaporation can be thinned by simply adding a bit of acetone or lacquer thinner—not paint thinner—and shaking well. In addition, it sets quickly, is inexpensive, and comes in a variety of colours.

I have used shellac, and while it gave no problems, it is not waterproof. Another disadvantage was that I could buy it only in a 10-ounce (284-millilitre) container or larger. Furthermore, I soon discovered that it was impractical to apply with a brush since it had to be constantly cleaned. A toothpick proved the best applicator. Very slow drying was another problem so I soon stopped using it.

Tip: When tying flies, it is not unusual to accidentally fill the hook eye with head cement. The cement will cause no problem if a small hackle feather is put butt first into the eye and drawn through while the cement is wet.

Chapter 4

Fly Hooks

Hooks for fly tying are manufactured in many styles, sizes, and wire weights. Most are made of steel, the quality as varied as the shapes and sizes. Although stainless steel and other alloys are used in hooks for special uses, they are not used in any quantity.

The parts of the hook are the eye, shank, bend, barb, and point. The distance between the shank and the point is known as the "gape"; that from the point to the bend is the "throat." There are many shapes, sizes, and combinations to suit special requirements.

A simple thing such as the hook eye, for example, has many shapes. The common ball eye is simply a ring made in the end of the shank, then turned down at a 45-degree angle. If it is not turned down it is called a "ringed" eye and is often handy for bait or lure use. The eye can also be turned up, a style favoured by Atlantic salmon fishers and some dry-fly trout fishers. The tapered eye, as the name implies, is thinned to a smaller diameter and therefore makes a less bulky eye. A looped eye is made by flattening the end of the wire, then forming the loop and bringing the flattened end along the shank a short distance. This makes for a bulky head, but these hooks are also favoured for Atlantic salmon flies and some steelhead flies.

Hook shanks are available in a variety of lengths and wire gauges. The most useful are standard length, 2X long, and 3X long. I have found the one-quarter and one-half longer to be of limited use. Because of the extreme length of the shank, fish seem able to get the leverage to throw the hook. Although I do not like hooks with such long shanks, there are fly patterns that cannot be dressed on shorter ones.

Hooks are made of regular round wire or forged wire. Many hooks made with round wire will straighten under pressure, making them useless for fishing. Forged hooks, on the other hand, are much stronger and a better choice for flies. In cross-section, forged wire is flattened on either side, reducing weight and increasing strength.

The bend of a hook is the subject of debate whenever fly tyers get together. Since the bend, the barb, and the point are the business end of a hook, each is discussed among fly tyers as fervently as a new baby is among neighbouring parents. The most useful bends on fly hooks are the round, sproat, and limerick.

The round bend seems to be the most popular, although the sproat is also a great favourite and has considerable merit. And while there are strong arguments in favour of the limerick, it is not as popular as the others. The round bend has the best penetration.

Some anglers feel that the sproat and the limerick bends, particularly the latter, are the most effective for avoiding the short strikes that are so annoying. The limerick, owing to its longer bend, extends the hook farther beyond the dressing. This extra length is thought to hook fish that would otherwise be a short strike. While I do not believe the theory, I feel it worthy of mention.

The sproat is a very good bend. For dry flies it permits tying the tail on at the proper angle to support the rear of the fly at a natural level on the water. In addition, it can be used to tie flies with curved bodies.

Hook points and barbs are treated as a unit and are important enough to be carefully examined. There is no value, however, in describing all types of points and barbs, as many have little importance to the fly tyer. The point most commonly seen on fly hooks is called "hollow ground needle point." The point is long, thinly tapered to a sharp barb, and hollowed on the gape side. Points that are not hollow ground appear short and stubby and require some force to get adequate penetration. Then there are those cut so close to the bend (throat) that the point's holding quality is limited, even with penetration. The reason is obvious—the hook cannot penetrate very far before being stopped by the bend.

Of interest to anglers who like to release fish is the barbless hook. It is designed with a sharp round point, the barb being simply a short, hump-like bend immediately behind the point where a normal barb would be. Simply pinching down the barb on a standard hook is, however, a more favoured approach.

Hook sizes refer to the gape, the distance from shank to point, without regard to the length of the hook. Sizes commonly used for trout flies are, from large to small, numbers 4, 6, 8, 10, 12, 14, 16,

Hooks Shown in Actual Size

8 Standard

94840 Standard Length

#10 2X Long

9671 2X Long

#12 3X Long

9672 3X Long

#14 4X Long

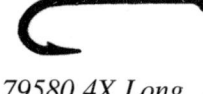

79580 4X Long

Round Bend

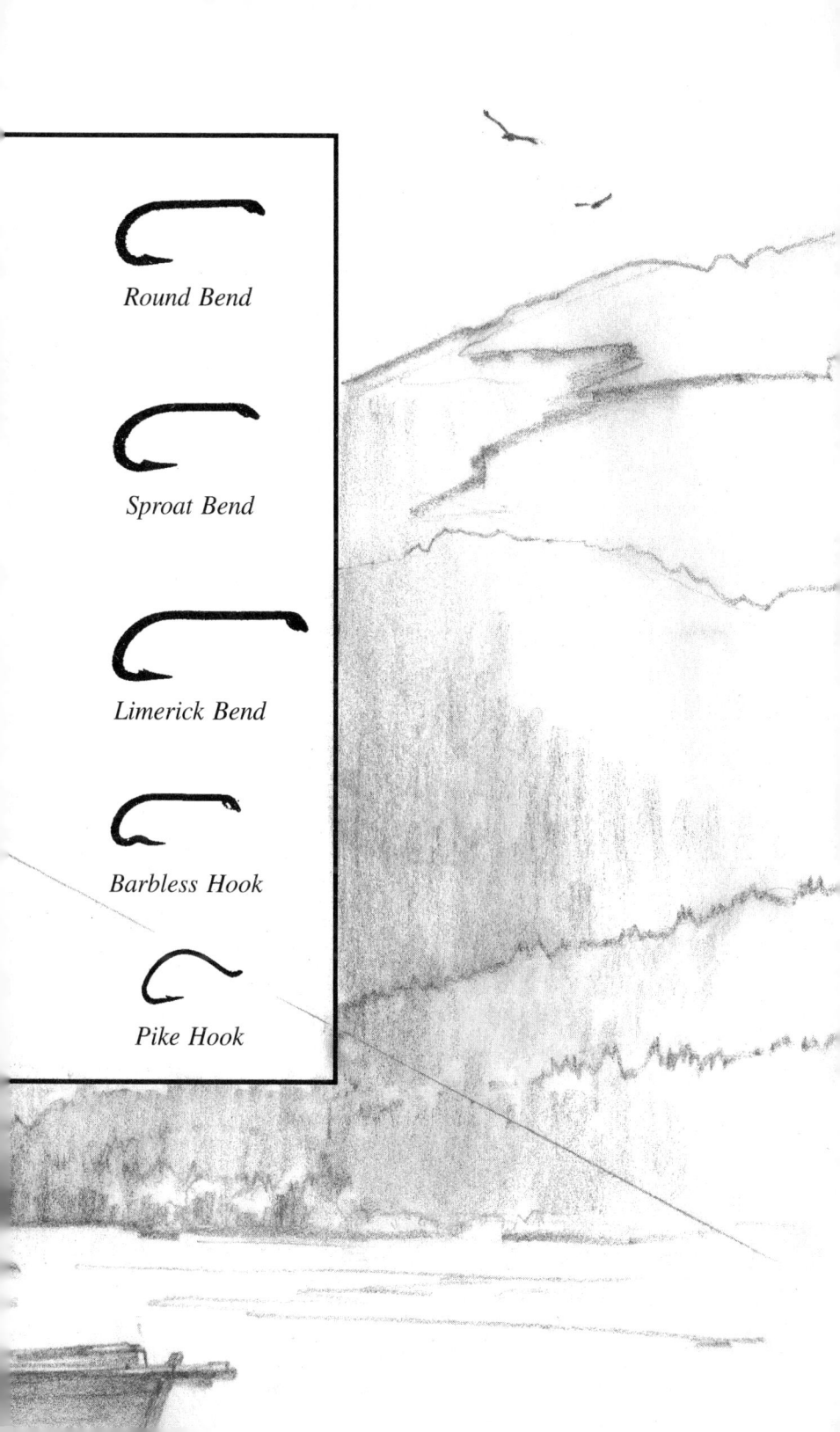

Sproat Bend

Limerick Bend

Barbless Hook

Pike Hook

and 18. Sizes 14, 16, 18, and smaller are usually only available in extra-fine wire. Specialty shops are the best source for them since these tiny hooks are not usually stocked in general sporting goods outlets. Hooks smaller than size 18 are not popular for fishing trout lakes.

You should always select a hook based on the fly pattern's ability to conceal it without sacrificing hooking efficiency. Some fly patterns call for large bodies while others require little dressing on the hook shank. The closer the barb and point can be kept to the shank (gape), the better the concealment of the bend, barb, and point will be. Soft, furry-bodied flies can be dressed on hooks with shallow gape, in many cases to near total concealment, owing to the compressibility of the body material. By contrast, the harder, large-bodied dressings require a deeper gape because the lack of compressibility seriously reduces the effective gape. Note that as gape size increases, the wire gets thicker and heavier.

A standard length hook of size 8 will have a shank approximately the same length as a size 10 (shallower gape) in a 2X long shank. A size 12, 3X long, and a size 14, 4X long, are close to the length of the standard size 8 and the gape will be progressively smaller. Most gape-to-shank lengths are related in the same way, permitting an almost unlimited selection of gape size to shank length.

Chapter 5

Tools and Fly-Tying Aids

Fly tying is an ancient art that traditionally required no tools other than scissors. Success depended entirely on the tyer's skill, and old-time tyers created flies every bit as good as those produced today. I'm extraordinarily impressed by some of their creations, but few people today have the patience and skill to dress flies in this difficult manner. Most are amazed that flies really could be produced without a vise and all our other now-standard tools. It's probably a good thing that tools have been developed and continually improved to make fly tying a skill almost anyone can practise. Modern tools greatly simplify the tying process and require no great investment.

Present-day fly tyers use such tools as a vise, hackle pliers, bobbin, whipfinisher, scissors, bodkin, hackle guard, material clips, knife, and dubbing hook. Other materials include waterproof coloured-ink pens, an art gum eraser, dubbing wax, and head cement. All these are useful and necessary to get the most enjoyment out of fly tying.

The **vise** is used to hold a hook securely in a convenient position. There are a great many models in a wide range of prices. The best have pointed jaws and angled head for convenience and comfort. On some models the head angle is fixed, while others have an adjustable angle. It is tiring to work on a vise with a horizontal head as it forces the hand into a strained position, so this type should be avoided. Others have flat-faced jaws and hold a hook securely in only one position. This model forces the tyer to work forward on the hook, thereby having far too much hook protruding to the rear of the fly's body. When you purchase a vise, test to ensure that it holds a hook securely in the desired position.

The shaft the vise's head is mounted on has a clamp on the lower end for fastening to a table or bench. On better vises the shaft

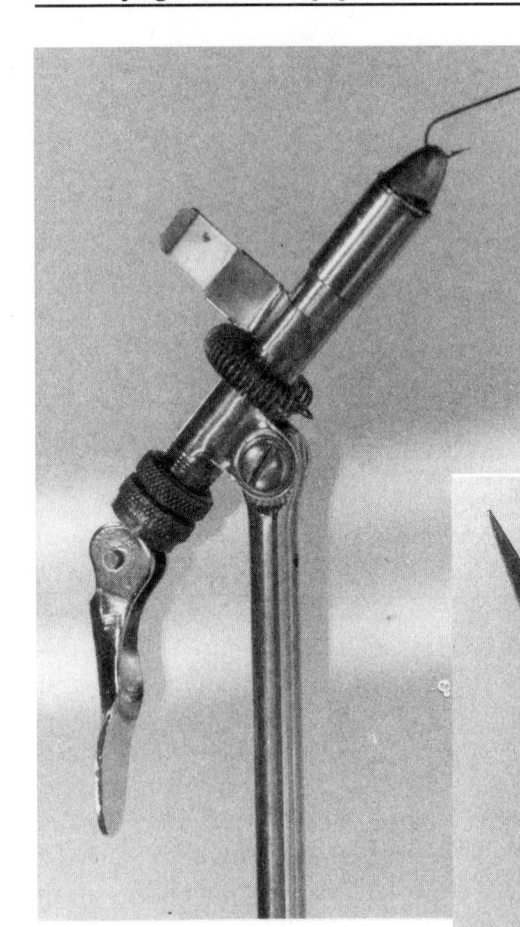

*Hook correctly
set in the vise.*

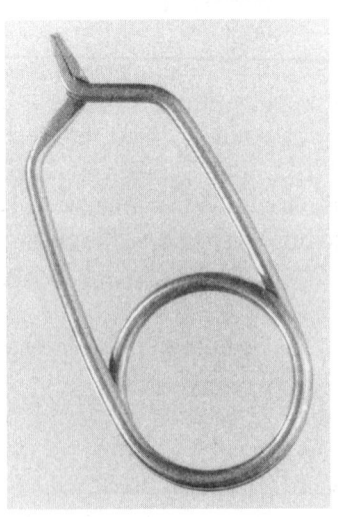

*Fly-tying scissors—
the tool most used.
The best is none too good.*

English hackle pliers

can be adjusted for height and left- or right-hand tying. On less expensive models, shaft and clamp are one piece, so there is no elevation adjustment and the vise cannot be easily clamped to a table or bench for left-handed tyers.

To get the most enjoyment, purchase the best vise you can afford. There is nothing more infuriating than to have a fly fall out when it is only partly dressed.

Hackle pliers are designed to hold hackle feathers while winding the feather onto a hook. They are also used for holding thread and tinsel out of the way, as well as for gripping body material, including ribbing material, during wrapping operations. The pliers are a simple tool, more like a small clamp than traditional pliers. There are many models, most of the same general design. I try to avoid those with rubber pads on the jaws. After a short time the natural oils in feathers attack the rubber. This makes the pliers continually slip off the feather, which is also infuriating!

The **bobbin** holds a spool of thread under adjustable tension. The thread is fed into the fine tube, then through onto the hook. Some tyers prefer to tie without a bobbin, but its use really does simplify things. By letting the tool hang by the thread while you perform other operations, you eliminate the need to use half hitches to hold the material in place. Bobbins also make it easy to apply thread in difficult areas of a hook, and they eliminate the need to cut and wax the correct length of thread required for each fly. It is most frustrating to miscalculate the length and find you've run out of thread just before you complete a complex fly.

There are many bobbin designs, but the simple wishbone models are efficient and inexpensive. They hold a regular spool of thread, so you don't need to run the thread onto a special spool. Since this model has fixed tension, the only way to make adjustments is to bend the legs slightly—in for more tension, out for less. The adjusting must be done with care or the tool can be ruined. Many models use springs of various design to apply tension to the thread.

Before purchasing a bobbin, examine carefully the ends of the tube through which the thread passes. Even the slightest roughness here will cause continual thread breakage. Avoid all models where the thread does not come directly off the spool into a straight tube.

There are a number of ways to thread a bobbin. A method that works well on most models is to double a piece of stiff, fine monofilament, feed it down the tube, put the end of the thread through the loop, then withdraw the monofilament, pulling the thread up through the tube. Where the thread can be fed into the lower end of the tube it is possible, with enough slack, to suck on the open upper end. This simple method draws the thread through quickly. Some of the more expensive models come equipped with a threading needle.

The **whipfinisher** is a tool used to tie off the thread at the fly's head. It is fast, accurate, and makes a secure tie. There are many models. All use the same principle, but some are superior in quality and design. The whipfinisher can be a troublesome piece of equipment to master, but by studying the illustrations on pages 56 to 59 and practising on a bare hook you will get the knack. If progress is slow, don't despair. In my classes, most students found the whipfinisher the most difficult piece of equipment to learn.

The tool most used by a fly dresser is **scissors**. While all other tools could be dispensed with, a good pair of sharp scissors is essential. The best is none too good. They have to cut to the point, which must be fine and sharp. They should not be over 5 inches (13 centimetres) long, with the eyes large enough for fingers to slip into easily. Straight blades are preferred over curved.

Another simple and useful tool is the **bodkin**. Most bodkins are just large darning needles with wood, plastic, or metal handles. Some have a fine wire protruding from the other end, about 1 inch (26 millimetres) long with a small loop in the end. The needle end is used to pick out hackle that may have been wound down, to clean cement from the hook eye, to pick out fur bodies to improve the fuzzy appearance, or to pick out hackle to represent legs. The small loop on the other end holds hackle out of the way when tying off the head. The user will no doubt find many more uses.

The **hackle guard** is also a simple tool. It resembles a small funnel with the spout cut off and a split down the side. It has a handle with a loop on the end. A short piece of string and a small

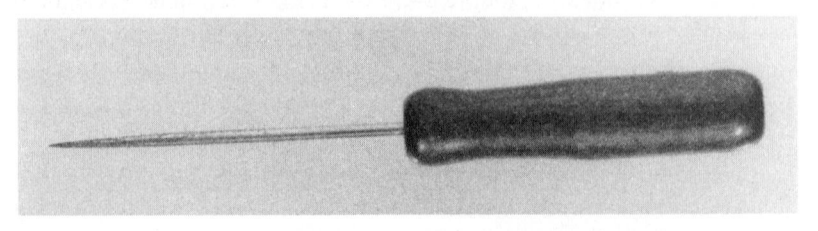

A bodkin is essentially a large darning needle.

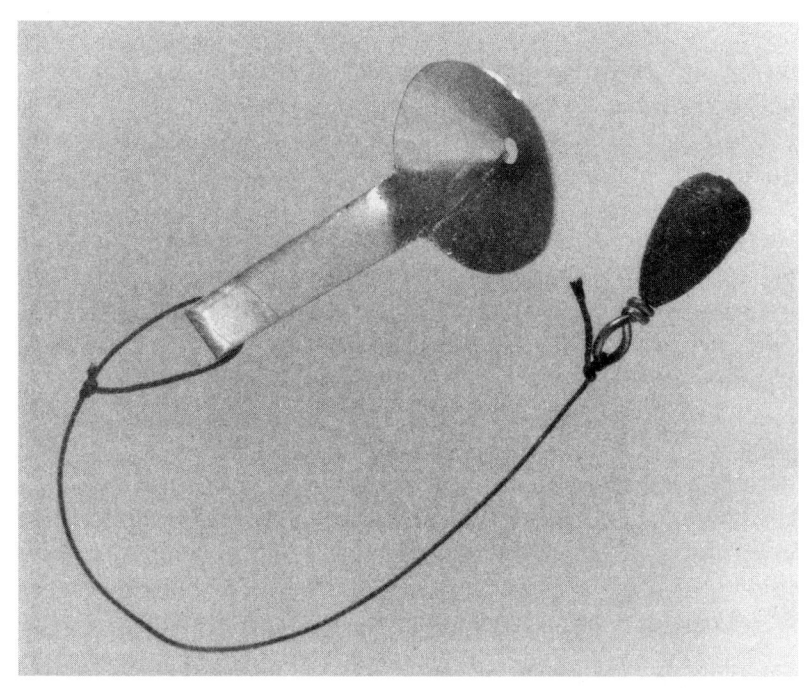

The hackle guard is a simple but handy tool.

weight complete it. In use, the string threads through a hole in the shaft, or pedestal, below the head on some of the more expensive vises. One end of the string attaches to the hackle guard handle, the other to a small, teardrop-shaped lead weight about a 1/2 inch (13 millimetres) long. To use the hackle guard, slip it over the hook eye with the thread passing through the slit in the side. This holds the hackle out of the way while the head is formed and the thread tied off and lacquered.

A **material clip** is designed to hold material out of the way while performing other operations. There are a number of models. The simplest and probably the most popular model clips on top of the vise. It is made of a double piece of spring steel, which is shaped on the lower end to clip onto the vise head. On the upper end the sides are flared to form a small trough that permits easy access for material. It is about 3/8 inch (10 millimetres) wide by about 1 1/2 inches (4 centimetres) long.

A model I like is a simple spring, 1 1/2 inches long and 1/4 inch (7 millimetres) in diameter, that wraps around the vise head. It is an expansion-type spring made from thin wire. Another more elaborate model has a rather weighty base designed to sit on the bench so it can be moved. It can also be adjusted for height. The upper end, which holds the material, is two rubber discs, slightly bevelled on the inner faces. It is designed primarily for holding material forward of the hook or off to the side.

A common tool used frequently is a **knife**. I like the small utility knife with a blade that retracts into the handle. Each blade has 12 sections; as the tip becomes dull it can be broken off and a new sharp section is ready. Extra blades come in packages of 10. This type of knife is inexpensive and carried by most hardware and department stores.

Tip: Magnetize your knife by rubbing it on a good magnet for a short time, and it will easily pick up small flies and hooks that have dropped or spilled.

Useful additions to a fly tyer's bench are **waterproof ink pens** in a selection of colours. When you need a length of coloured thread to rib a fly, a section of white thread can be quickly changed to the desired colour. For instance, if you need maroon, simply run a blue pen over the thread, followed by a red one. In this way a great many variations are possible with only a few basic colours. You will discover many uses for these pens, in both broad and pointed nib. I like Pantone by Letraset, mostly because of its wide range of colours. Art stores carry these pens.

An **art gum eraser**, or any soft rubber eraser, is most useful to remove the flue from peacock herl. Many small nymph, pupae, and dry-fly patterns call for stripped herl. By simply running the herl over the eraser, or vice versa, it is easy to completely remove the flue.

A wide range of other items generally used for other purposes can aid the fly tyer. A paper muffin cup, for example, would seem of no tying value, but it is just what you need when dubbing wax becomes hard and unusable, which is a standard problem. Reconstitute the wax by putting it in a small metal container and then putting wax and container into boiling water. (Do not put the wax directly on the heat—it is extremely flammable and therefore dangerous.) When it's thoroughly melted, carefully pour the wax into a small paper muffin cup and let it cool. Then put it in the freezer until it is completely frozen. Now you can easily remove it from the paper.

Tinsel-Making Machine

A fly tyer frequently wants special tinsel that is not commercially available. I, for example, like copper tinsel but have never seen it offered for sale. To solve my problem a friend made a machine for me. It is not fancy but works perfectly on both the fine copper wire from the armature of an electric shaver and the heavier wire strands in appliance cords. It can also turn fine gold (brass) and silver wire into good-quality tinsel. I can clamp the machine in a bench vise and run off 15 to 20 feet (5 to 6 metres) of flat tinsel in a few minutes. Then I roll it onto an empty thread spool.

The machine is easy to make. For the body use a steel plate about 1/3 inch (8 millimetres) thick, 3 inches (8 centimetres) wide, and 6 inches (15 centimetres) long. For the anvil, use two ball

Homemade tinsel-making machine.

bearings about 2 inches (5 centimetres) in diameter and 3/4 inch (20 millimetres) wide. Press each of the ball bearings onto a short shaft, then face them flat and smooth in a lathe. Drill a 3/8-inch (10-millimetre) hole in the centre of each shaft for the bolt, then drill the plate.

With the faces of the rims together, measure the distance between the holes, centre to centre, then drill both holes. One hole, preferably the top, should be slightly longer each way, up and down, so that there can be some adjustment of pressure on the wire. Weld a short piece of steel rod to the outside rim of the lower bearing as a handle. Be careful not to mar the surface of the flange that will be the anvil. To make good quality tinsel the two surfaces must be glassy smooth.

Mount the lower bearing, the one with the handle, first. It goes in the round hole; the other goes in the elongated hole.

Tighten the bottom bolt first, really tight. Then tighten the top, but not so tight it cannot be moved with a clout from a hammer. With the machine clamped in the vise, run a piece of your wire between the two bearings. Tap the nut side of the top bolt either up or down until the tinsel is to your liking. Then firmly tighten the top nut.

Bolts with a fine thread (SAE) will stay tight better than a coarse thread (US).

Although my machine is designed for clamping to a vise, it can be easily modified for a bench top by welding a flange to the lower end to take a "C" clamp. Remember to keep the faces of the bearings clean and unmarked and you will have many years of satisfaction.

The CO_2 Cartridge Bobbin

When tying small flies—sizes 12, 14, 16, 18—I found the Thompson bobbin I use much too heavy. It often bent the hook when I left it hanging. I tried other bobbins, but all were either bulky or would catch material and tangle it when the bobbin was hanging. After a lot of thought I decided to make my own and it has proven a great success. It is small, light, and compact, with little projecting to catch material and tangle when left hanging. I now have a number of homemade bobbins with a different colour thread on each. This system saves time when I want to change colours or use more than one thread.

The bobbin is made from an empty pellet gun CO_2 cartridge. The brass tubing comes in 11-inch (28-centimetre) lengths and should be about 1/16 inch (2 millimetres) inside diameter. A fine

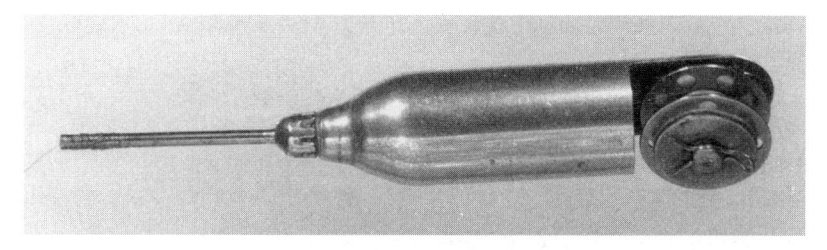

Bobbin made from CO$_2$ cartridge

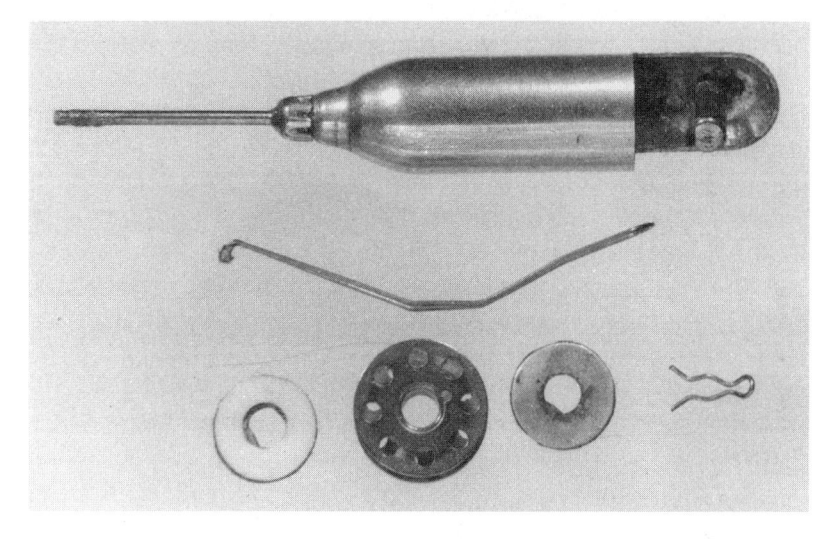

Exploded view of bobbin made by the author from a CO$_2$ cartridge.

steel wire about the same diameter as the butt end of a tapered leader and some 3 feet (90 centimetres) long will make the spring. Brass brazing rod about 7/32 inches (6 millimetres) in diameter and 3 feet long makes the shaft. The brass tubing and steel wire are available at most good hobby shops; the brazing rod at a machine shop or welding supply house. The spool is a narrow shuttle bobbin for a Singer sewing machine, available at most notion counters in packs of four or six.

Completing the material list is a small piece of scrap sheet metal, about 22 gauge, and a piece of thin Teflon or plastic from a bleach jug or something similar to make friction washers.

Begin construction by cutting a length off the brass tubing about 3 inches (7 centimetres) long. This is the most important and difficult part. The ends have to be perfectly smooth or the thread will be continually broken, and once installed in the cylinder it is extremely difficult to correct.

You need a piece of fine emery cloth, a piece of ruby cloth (a super-fine abrasive cloth, reddish in colour), a square piece of scrap leather, some automobile simonize cutting compound, and a small electric drill.

With a small twist drill (a hand drill, not power) and a small fine file, round off the inside and outside edges on both ends of the tube. Put it in the drill and with the fine emery cloth lying on a soft backing, lightly hold the tube vertical with the end pressed on the emery cloth. Then repeat the operation on the ruby cloth. Every few rotations put the tube down in a different place, rolling the drill around slightly all the time. Generously rub some cutting compound into the leather and then, in the same way as with the emery cloth, polish the ends on the leather, frequently putting the tube in a new location. When you think it is smooth enough, clean it inside and out. Then suck a short piece of tying thread through the tube and, holding it at right angles, swing the tube around a number of times. If the thread remains unfrayed, do the same at the other end. If the thread frays, repeat the polishing process.

After the tube is completed, start on the cylinder. Centre punch the base and drill in both ends holes the same size as the outer diameter of the tube. Take a length of steel rod or wire that is about 6 inches (15 centimetres) long and that will fit snugly inside the tube, and bruise it with a hammer without bending it—this will prevent the tube from sliding more than its length down the rod. This rod is to hold the tube in place, straight and of the correct length while it is being soldered.

With the full length of the tube on the rod, kept there by the bruise, put the rod in the top of the cylinder and out the bottom until only 1 3/8 inches (35 millimetres) of the tube is protruding from the cylinder. Clean the top of the cylinder and the tube, then solder the tube in place. (Tinning the part of the tube to be soldered before assembly makes a better joint.) When cooled, pull the rod out through the bottom hole.

The next step is to prepare the area where the spool goes. With the cylinder held securely in the vise in a horizontal position, measure 1 inch (26 millimetres) from the bottom end. With a hacksaw, make a cut at right angles to the central axis of the cylinder, 19/32 inches (15 millimetres) deep. Then make another cut parallel to the central axis from the bottom to the ends of the previous cut. Discard the resulting piece of metal. With a small half-round file, straighten both cuts and smooth all the edges. Wash any oil, filings, or other debris out of the cylinder with solvent.

In the middle of the remaining section of the base, centre punch a mark 15/32 inches (12 millimetres) from the end and drill a hole about the same diameter as the tube. (Size of this hole is not critical. It is only to hold the axle in an upright position while it is being soldered.) Remove any burring around the hole, clean it with steel wool or emery cloth, then tin the area so that it solders without any problem.

From the brazing rod cut a piece about 2 inches (5 centimetres) long and file the ends smooth. Since I don't have a metal lathe, I use my 1/4 inch (7 millimetre) drill held in a bench vise—firmly, but not too tight or the drill will be damaged.

Put the short piece of rod in the drill. Then, with the drill running, use a file to turn a section about 3/16 inch (5 millimetres) long to snugly fit the axle hole. From the shoulder of the turned section, measure 5/8 inch (16 millimetres). With the drill running, use a hacksaw to make a kerf for a clip to keep bobbin and washers in place. Cut the rod off about 1/16 inch (2 millimetres) above the kerf. Then put the axle piece in the vise, cut-off end out, and file smooth the end and edges of the kerf. At this point check to ensure that the wire for the clip will fit easily into the kerf. With the file take 1/16 inch (2 millimetres) off the side of the axle to keep the friction washers from turning when a hole is punched in the washers to match this half-moon configuration of the axle. Make sure the bobbin fits easily on the shaft and turns smoothly. At times I find it necessary to clean the hole in the spool because it is uneven and catches the edge of the flat area on the shaft. A small round chain-saw file is perfect for this job.

With the cylinder in the vise ready to take the axle, file the axle shoulders to fit the curve of the cylinder. With the flat area facing the tube end, and with the shaft plumb to either side and leaning slightly towards the tube end, solder it in place. Then cut the waste end off the other side and file and sand it smooth.

The friction device is made of two washers faced with thin Teflon or plastic. To work properly they must fit with a little slack, but not so much that they are able to turn on the axle.

I made a punch out of a used chain-saw file, snapping it off at a suitable length, then grinding the ends flat and smooth. One end I ground to the same shape as the axle and slightly larger because when the metal is punched it becomes slightly concave. When it is flattened, the hole becomes a bit smaller and the punch will not fit the shaft. When grinding the punch, keep trying until you get a good fit. Place the metal on a piece of wood or whatever is suitable and punch in the holes. Then turn the metal over and flatten the bulges. The washer, when finished, should be 1/16 inch (2 millimetres) smaller than the spool's diameter all the way round. Make the friction washer out of Teflon or plastic bleach bottle or similar material. Then glue it on the washers and trim the edges.

The clip is made by driving three nails into the edge of a short piece of 2 x 4, 3/32 inch (3 millimetres) apart in a straight line. Use a 3-inch (7.6-centimetre) nail in the middle and 2 1/4-inch (5.7-centimetre) nails on either side. Pre-drill the holes slightly smaller than the nails, drive the nails in only part way, and cut them off so that they stick out about 1/4 inch (6 millimetres). File the ends smooth and you have an efficient jig on which you can make any number of identical clips.

Double a piece of steel wire about 2 1/2 inches (6 centimetres) long and place it over the three nails. With a pair of small ringing or needle-nose pliers, squeeze the wire together between the first two nails. Hold the squeezed wire and with another pair of pliers pinch it together between the next two nails. Should you not have a second pair of pliers, a small finishing nail on either side will hold the wire in place while it is pinched between the next two nails. Remove it from the nails and cut off the waste. The round end can be bent up a bit to make it easier to remove and replace when required.

The spring is made from the steel wire. A piece about 8 inches (20 centimetres) long is bent double in the middle around a rod or bolt 5/16 inch (8 millimetres) in diameter. It is easy if a simple jig is made by drilling a hole a bit smaller in a piece of wood and driving the rod or bolt into it. Then 3 inches (7.6 centimetres) away, drive a nail that is slightly larger in diameter than the tube, measuring from outside to outside. With the wire around the larger rod and the sides straight, wrap the other two ends around the smaller one to fit closely. The ends should form two half circles, one on top of the other. With side cutters, cut off the excess wire.

Holding these half circles tightly on top of each other, solder them together. Bend the wire as shown in the photo on page 37 to complete the spring. The narrow end fits under the tube and the wide end over the axle. Place a friction washer on top of the spring with the Teflon or plastic up, then put in the sewing machine spool. The other washer goes on top of the spool, plastic down. Then clip in place to complete the bobbin.

All that remains is to load the spool (use a drill, sewing machine, or adapt any small motor) and adjust the tension to suit by bending the spring slightly or adding an additional washer.

You will need a threader to get the thread through the tube. It is made from 8-pound (4-kilogram) test monofilament. When doubled, it should be about 8 inches (20 centimetres) long. Knot the two ends together, then wrap with some red tape so you can easily find it on your tying bench. To use, feed the monofilament down the tube from the outer end, double end first, put the thread through the loop, and draw it up the tube.

Carding Brushes

Carding brushes are used in pairs to blend all types of fur and wool. They make it simple and convenient to blend different colours, producing a wide range of shades and tones. A length of wool cut into 2-inch (5-centimetre) pieces quickly becomes a ball of fluffy dubbing material.

The genuine carding brushes used by our grandparents are fairly large, about 5 by 9 inches (12 by 23 centimetres). Each brush is a pad of leather studded with rows of wire teeth curved towards the handle. They are used one in each hand. Place the wool on one brush, put the other on top, and pull in opposite directions. Pulling with both handles in the same direction, alternating the brushes, puts the material into a loose roll. Work it until the desired texture or shade is attained.

Although some animal grooming brushes can be used, they are much smaller, with longer and thinner teeth. As a consequence, they are not nearly as strong. The best place to buy carding brushes is a wool craft store.

Velcro Brush

It is often desirable to comb a dubbed body. For this purpose I use a simple tool made from a discarded toothbrush. Cut the bristles off the supporting material and then sandpaper or scrape until it provides a good base for adhesive. Cut a piece off the hook side of a section

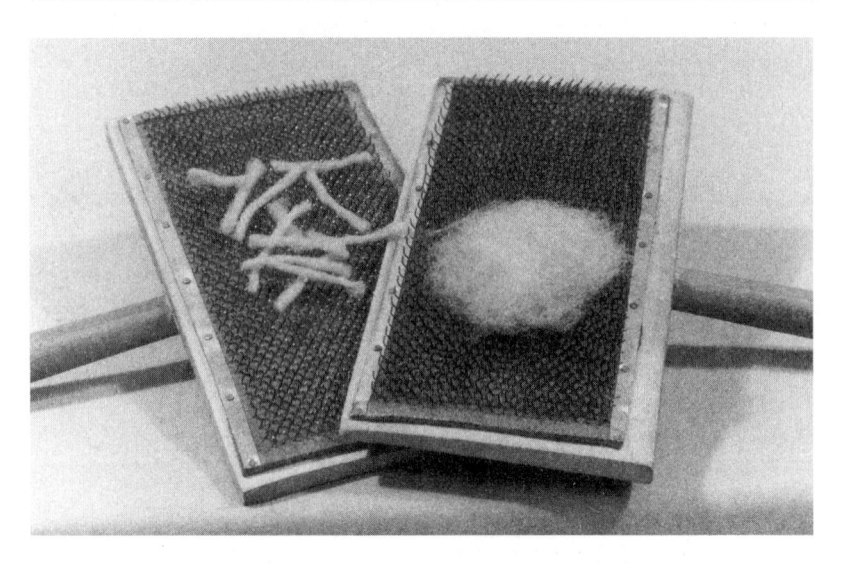

Carding brushes—with material ready to card and carded.

of Velcro to cover where the bristles were. Attach the Velcro with contact cement and trim off the waste. For the brush to function properly, be sure that the Velcro hook curves towards the handle when the brush is pulled towards you.

Setting Fur and Feathers

Flies dressed with long hair and/or feathers often appear rough and messy because the material doesn't stay in place, even when you pick out the wild hair or feathers, press them, or twist them. A winged fly will often give similar problems. A remedy that is frequently successful is to soak the fly for a few seconds in very hot water to which you have added a bit of wetting agent such as Kodak Photo Flo (no odour) or dishwashing detergent. After soaking, comb or stroke into the desired appearance, mount by the hook on a piece of Styrofoam, and let dry.

A winged fly, after being teased into shape, should be carefully placed in a shallow cup or tumbler until dry, with the top of the wing against the outer circumference of the cup. Then preen it gently with your fingers to separate any fibres that may be sticking. With reasonable care the fly will maintain its shape for many seasons.

Tools and Fly-Tying Aids 43

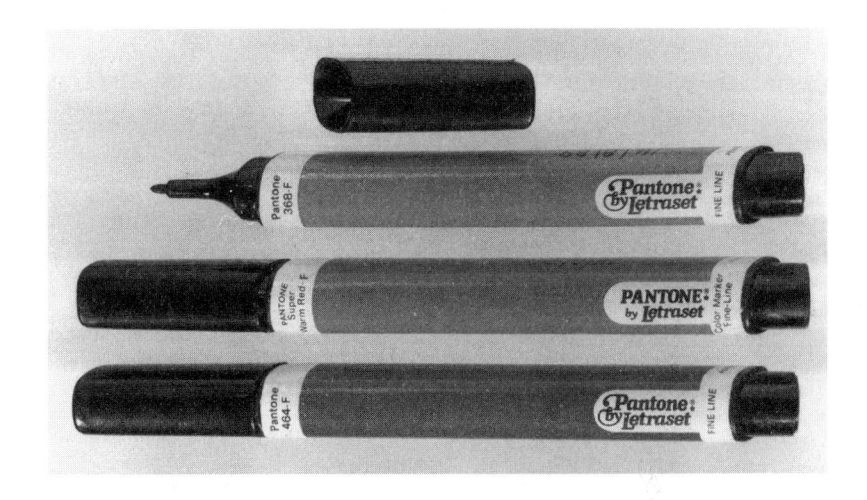

Waterproof ink pens are useful for quickly changing white thread to various colours.

Setting wet fly wings when wet.

Needle threader.

Rejuvenating Flies and Feathers

Flies that become misshapen because they were stored wet or carelessly dropped in a fly box will not perform well. When retrieved they frequently spin or otherwise act in an unnatural manner. You can, however, restore them to their original condition—or even to a superior state. Bring a kettle to a rolling boil and, with forceps, hold the fly in the steam from the spout for a few seconds. It will regain its original shape. If the original shape is not satisfactory it can, to some degree, be changed with the hot-water treatment described in the previous section, "Setting Fur and Feathers."

Curling Feathers and Fur

There are times when it is desirable to curve a feather. The tails of dry mayflies and shrimp are two instances, and doubtless many others will arise during fly tying.

The curving is done with your thumbnail, dubbing needle, and the back of a knife blade or pair of scissors, in conjunction with the first joint of your thumb. Place your thumbnail on the side to which you want the fibres to curve, then put the fleshy part of the first joint of your index finger on the underside as an anvil. With light to moderate pressure on the fibres, draw your thumbnail along them from base to tip in a curling motion. Adjusting the pressure controls the degree of curl.

The dubbing needle or knife blade is used in a similar manner. Hold the tool in your hand so that it crosses the fleshy part of the first joint of your thumb, which becomes the anvil.

Dyeing Your Own Material

When the material you need is not available in the desired colour or shade, dyeing your own material is the solution. It is simple, the cost is small, and the equipment and material (except the dye) are in the average kitchen. One word of caution—don't use the cook's favourite pot, particularly if it is aluminum. The acid dyes stain and it is difficult, if not impossible, to clean the utensil.

You will need:
- two bowls—the size depending on the volume to be dyed,
- a large spoon,
- a cooking pot,

Tools and Fly-Tying Aids   45

- dye,
- paper towels,
- a small spoon,
- a wire strainer about 4 inches (10 centimetres) in diameter,
- lots of old newspaper to work on,
- a wetting agent such as a liquid detergent or Kodak's Photo Flo,
- salt, preferably coarse pickling salt since table salt contains additives,
- any kind of vinegar, and
- a sample colour. Don't try to remember a colour; it cannot be done accurately.

Always work in daylight. Fluorescent light casts a greenish tinge and tungsten light an orange colour, so making an accurate colour comparison under these light sources is virtually impossible. Any artificial light must have a colour temperature of 5500 degrees Kelvin, the colour temperature of daylight. As already noted, fluorescent tubes that produce this temperature are VITA-LITE's 40-watt, Duro-Test 33,000-hour, double cathodes.

To start the dyeing process put the required volume of water in a pan, add salt in the proportion of 1 tablespoon (15 millilitres) to one quart (just over one litre) of water, and add dye. Colours can be mixed to obtain others. For example, yellow and blue make green, red and blue become maroon, and so forth throughout the colour spectrum.

In one bowl put one quart (just over one litre) of water, preferably hot, to which add 1/2 teaspoon (2.5 millilitres) of wetting agent. In the second bowl put one quart (just over one litre) of cold water and add 2 tablespoons (30 millilitres) of vinegar. In the wetting agent, thoroughly soak the material to be dyed. Drain.

Take a small piece of the material to be dyed and test the dye bath for strength. (Always make the dye bath weak to start, and bring it up to strength.) If you have to strengthen the bath after the material has been put in, remove the material before adding more dye. Follow the directions on the package for temperature, etc. When you have the material satisfactorily dyed, let it drain for a few minutes before putting it in the vinegar bath. Leave it in the vinegar for 10 minutes or so to help set the dye. After the vinegar bath, rinse that material in cold water until the water runs clear, then spread it out to dry. When it's thoroughly dried it may need fluffing up—loose hackle feathers give the most trouble in this regard. They are best put in a cloth bag with lots of room. Close the bag and shake it vigorously for a few minutes. That will usually bring them into shape.

The dyes I have used are Tintex, Rit, and Ampollina. Rit and Tintex are available in most supermarkets and pharmacies; Ampollina, in hobby shops. While all are satisfactory products, there is some variance in colours, so it is a matter of choice. Should you be interested in natural dyes from grass, berries, flowers, and other flora, your library can supply detailed information.

I find that most commercial dyes are too brilliant. To muddy them—"sadden" them it is called—put a touch of black into the dye bath with the end of a wooden toothpick. Use extreme care, however, because even a bit too much will ruin the colour.

Bleaching Natural Materials

When dyeing natural fur, hair, and feathers, it's often hard to obtain the desired colours because the material is too dark. The usual types of bleaching agents such as peroxide or washing bleach either do not work or seem to burn the material, reducing it to a dead, lifeless state.

I have found a way to successfully reduce the darkness in quills, hackle feathers, beaver fur, black bear hair, and deer hair to the shade I need. In some cases the remaining natural colour has imparted a slightly muddy tone, but I have not found this condition objectionable since it reduces the harsh, unnatural brilliance of manufactured dyes.

The bleaching agent I use is "Born Blonde," by L'Oreal, which I found in the hair-care section of the local pharmacy. As an example of its effectiveness, I treated a patch of really black, black-bear hide with the solution and it was transformed into a beautiful, glossy, light oak colour. I also treated a section of rich brown beaver fur, then dyed it insect green, and it became a natural, slightly muddy, insect green colour.

For advice on bleaches that might remove more colour than "Born Blonde," you might find it worthwhile to visit the local hair stylist, especially if he or she fly fishes. Perhaps flies can be swapped for information.

Chapter 6

Dubbing

Dubbing is any fur-like material that can be spun on a thread and wrapped on a hook to form a fly body. It can be natural fur, hair, or fine synthetic fibres, either pure or mixed, in any number of colours that can also be solid or mixed. Mixed fibres, natural and synthetic, create interesting textures and effects. Similarly, colours mixed with carding brushes can produce interesting and useful shades and tones.

There are many ways to make dubbing. Some tyers simply rub fur onto their waxed thread. Others form a loop of waxed thread and twist it into a dubbing strand with their fingers. Feel free to try any of the various dubbing techniques, but I recommend using a dubbing hook and the method that follows.

Dubbing hooks are made in a number of styles. The best are about 4 inches (10 centimetres) long and shaped like a miniature shepherd's crook. One can be made from a piece of wire or an old #15 or #16 crochet hook. Simply break off the hook and bend the rest into the desired shape. A piece of soft plastic tube 2 inches (5 centimetres) long that you slip over the handle portion completes this simple tool.

Dubbing must be made into a chenille-like strand before it is durable enough to be wrapped on a hook. On a single waxed thread it makes a body that looks satisfactory but is not durable and soon pulls apart. The most durable dubbing is placed between two strands of thread, then twisted into a strand that, when finished, looks like a strand of chenille. You can easily make a strand of the size, colour, quantity, and texture that you require. Should the strand be too short, it is simple to continue from where the first one ends and keep going to any length. Should a colour change be desired, you can make the dubbing as short or as long as needed, with each section a different colour, size, texture, or material.

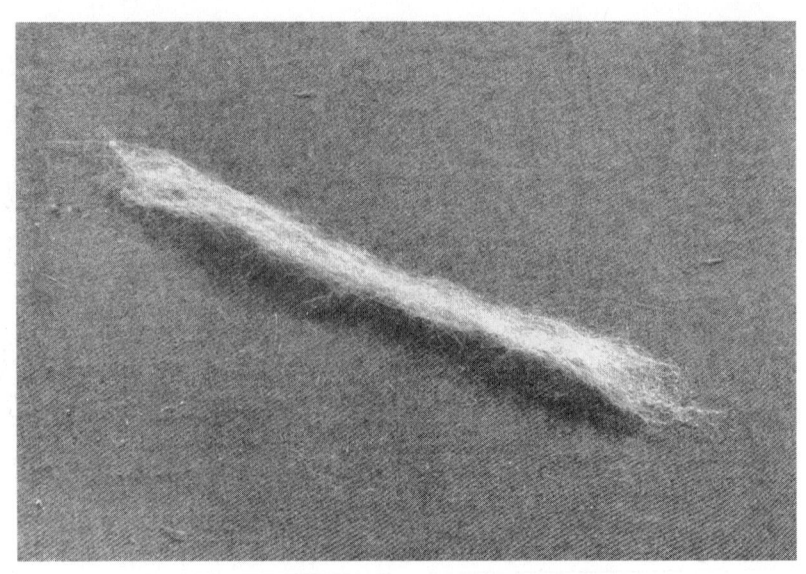

Strand of dubbing on dubbing board.

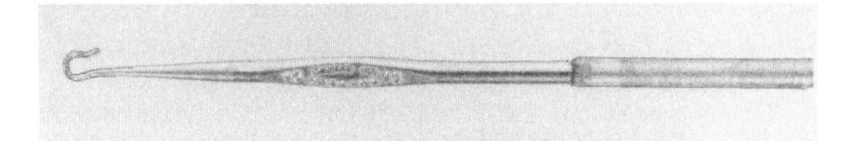

Dubbing hook.

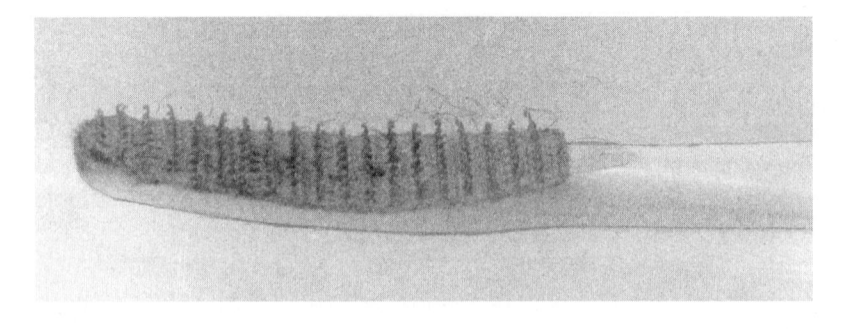

Dubbing brush.

In order to make a strand of dubbing, lay out the material where it can be worked into a long row, as thick as required. Short rows are more easily handled, and on long hooks it is easier to use two short strands than an unwieldy long one.

You can spread the row of dubbing on any surface—pant legs are popular—but it's best to use what I call a "dubbing board." It is simply a piece of plywood about 5/8 by 6 inches (16 millimetres by 15 centimetres), with a piece of cotton cloth stapled or glued to the top. The dubbing material is placed on the board and then teased into a row of the desired length and thickness.

In making dubbing, caution is beneficial. There is always a tendency to use far more material than necessary. Not only is this practice wasteful, but the dubbing is difficult to handle when it is bulkier than it has to be.

When the dubbing material is ready, wax the thread. With the thread started on the hook and wrapped to the bend, pull about 6 inches (15 centimetres) of thread off the bobbin and wax the entire length. Hold the bobbin in the left hand, and with the right carefully pick up the dubbing and place it on the half of the thread that is closest to the hook. Keep the end resting on the hook shank to help prevent it from rolling to the under side of the thread.

With the dubbing hook, catch the thread at the end of the dubbing, then lay the bare thread over on top. Gently place the bobbin over on to the far side of the hook and change hands.

Holding the hook in the left hand, the bobbin in the right, in spaced turns run the thread to the eye and let the bobbin hang. Turn the dubbing hook eight or ten times counter-clockwise until the material is firmly twisted into a chenille-like strand. Pick out any lumps and, if required, thin the strand by pulling material from the length. It can now be picked out with the dubbing needle, brushed with a Velcro brush, or trimmed with scissors.

Note: Whenever possible, use a thread similar in colour to the dubbing.

Chapter 7

Problems of a Novice Fly Tyer

During the many years I taught fly tying, I discovered that each class had the same problems. I also learned that it was easier for class members to solve problems when forewarned that they would probably arise. The following paragraphs describe a few of these problems.

Placing the Hook in the Vise

When a hook is placed in the vise, it is best to keep the point and barb clear of the jaw. If, as some tyers advocate, the jaw covers the point, the pressure will frequently fracture the hook just behind the barb. Then, too often, the point will drop off when the hook is released from the vise. Much worse, it can easily break in a fish. Those who favour covering the point argue that an exposed point will catch material as it is being wound around the hook. In addition, fingers can be jabbed on an uncovered point.

I have found, however, that fingers are pricked only a few times before one learns better. The same is true of material catching on the hook point. I'm therefore convinced that the hook should be set in the vise, point exposed, at about a 15-degree angle, the eye higher than the bend. With this positioning, the thread is unlikely to slip off over the eye when the bobbin is left to hang behind the eye during other operations.

Starting the Thread on the Hook

The beginner frequently has difficulty starting the thread on a hook. The following steps make starting extremely simple: Brush a little head cement or lacquer—as noted, I use clear fingernail polish—on the hook shank, then with about 4 inches (10 centimetres) of

Problems of a Novice Fly Tyer 51

Starting the thread on a hook.

Preparing to run the thread down the hook.

thread extending beyond the bobbin needle, hold the loose end in the left hand. Lay the thread across the hook shank at right angles close to the eye, the bobbin on the far side. Hold the thread by the end on your side of the hook, and hold the bobbin on the far side. By moving the bobbin clockwise, wrap the thread three times around the hook shank. On the fourth and succeeding wraps force the thread back over the previous turns, holding the loose portion in the left hand until the start of the bend is reached. The turns down the hook shank need not be close together. Take a few extra turns, then clip the remaining loose end as close as possible to the hook. Now let the bobbin hang and you are ready to start tying.

Making the Tail

Making tails too long is a common problem. The reason is that the material is held in the left hand, hiding the portion that will extend beyond the hook bend to form the tail. To overcome this problem, hold the material in the right hand on top of the hook shank. The length of the tail now can be seen and adjusted. Usually it should be no longer than the gape of the hook. Without moving the material, change hands. You are now ready to tie it down.

Here another difficulty arises: the material might revolve around the hook, or partly so, as the thread is wrapped. To avoid this problem, grasp the material and the hook shank firmly with thumb and first finger, applying pressure more with the ball of the finger and thumb than the tips. Bring the thread up under the tip of the thumb, then roll the pressure to the tip, thus trapping the thread. Now carry the thread loosely over the top and under the fingertip, again rolling the pressure forward to trap the thread. Holding the pressure against the thread on either side, pull down, drawing the thread tight over the tail material. Repeat three or four times. The tail should now be tied firmly in place on top of the hook shank. If it has rolled around the shank or partly so, it may be because you were keeping the thread too taut as it was brought over the top. This tautness forces the material ahead of the thread, carrying it around the hook shank. But cheer up. With a little practice this technique becomes simple and is applicable to all materials being tied on as tails or wings.

Making the Body

In applying body material, proportion and placement are common problems. Ideally, a body should start directly above the rear of the barb and end at some point behind the eye of the hook. The latter point is a matter of some judgment, governed by what is to be done with wings, hackle, or head. While most patterns require about 1/8 inch (3 millimetres) of space left behind the eye, large-headed nymphs such as dragonfly and damselfly will require up to 3/16 inch (5 millimetres). Therefore, consider carefully what dressing will be used other than body. Then allow the necessary space behind the eye when body material is tied off. Only with experience can you accurately gauge the space necessary to comfortably accommodate the material.

Too little room leads to crowding of the head, forcing you to come back over material such as body and hackle already in place. As a result, the hackle is forced back, often lying flat against the body. The result is an extremely large head, which makes it difficult, if not impossible, to tie the fly off. Also, it partly conceals the hook eye, causing extreme difficulty when you are tying the fly to a leader.

But perhaps this problem isn't all bad. A fishing companion once told me, "When I go fishing in the evening with anyone in my boat and I supply the flies, I give him one on which I've crowded the eye. Oh, man! I can sure get a lot of fishing done before he gets that fly tied on."

Most hackles, to be properly proportioned, should not quite reach the hook point. Only on special patterns, or to create a particular effect or representation, should they be longer or shorter.

Tying on Wings

Tying on wings always gives a great deal of trouble. Even most commercial tyers seem to have difficulty with this operation. Seldom is there a commercially tied fly with properly cocked wings. They often curve left or right, the result of improperly matched quills from which the feather was taken. Also, on wet flies the wings are often cocked too high, the result of improper thread tension when they were tied.

In securing wings, the first half dozen turns of the thread should be tight and firm. Then, as the thread is worked towards the rear on the final three or four turns, pressure should be decreased. If the thread is again brought forward, as it should be to form the head, gradually increase pressure as the thread comes toward the eye.

I've already mentioned, but it's worth repeating, that to make good wings a pair of quills, one from the right and one from the left side of the bird, are used. They should then curve in opposite directions and be matched for modelling and colour. As also mentioned, when both wing sections are taken from a single quill, they curve one way and cause a fly to spin as it is retrieved.

Tie wings on so they sit nicely on top of the hook, are of the correct length, and are properly cocked—this refers to the angle in relation to the body plane. Wet flies, dry flies, spent wing, etc., all have a particular angle at which the wings should be set. Getting the right angle can be troublesome and takes practice.

After selecting and matching the feathers, hold the butts together in the right hand and place them in position on top of the hook at the desired length. The length is usually the same as the body or a bit longer. Then change hands, with the tips of finger and thumb covering the hook eye. As you did when tying on the tail, roll the pressure back on finger and thumb to just back of the tips. Bring the thread up and trap it by rolling the pressure to the tip of the thumb. Then take the thread loosely over the top and down the far side, trapping the thread with the fingertip. It is now imperative that the finger and thumb be squeezed together very tightly. Pull down firmly on the thread without releasing pressure between finger and thumb; just roll them back, then forward again as the thread passes under the tips. Repeat for three or four wraps. Do not be tempted to release the pressure and peek. The wing will roll over immediately after pressure is relaxed.

When the required wraps have been made, release the pressure slightly and slide the fingers back on the wing to expose the area where it is tied. Place a drop of head cement on the tie, then immediately add three or four more turns of thread. Make a few light turns behind the last turns that hold the wing on to hold the wing cocked in the position you want. Loose turns will hold the wing down; tight turns force the wing tips up. Should the wings come down the sides of the hook shank, or if they roll onto their sides on top of the hook, the cause is likely insufficient pressure on the sides as the thread was tightened, or a release of pressure when you peeked at the wraps.

Wings present one other problem, although it is probably more the fault of some fly tyers, of which I am one. No matter how perfectly I hold the wings aligned on the hook, the finished fly will have them cocked to the far side and lying over slightly. The only solution that I have found is to allow for it by holding them to the opposite side and tilted slightly towards me.

Keeping the Right Bobbin Tension

Many students have a problem with the bobbin's thread tension being too loose. This looseness permits the thread between the bobbin needle and the hook to become so long it is unwieldy. There is then a tendency to wrap the thread with the fingers without the advantage of the bobbin. You can prevent the problem by keeping the distance from bobbin to hook short. That distance should at no time exceed 3/4 to 1 1/2 inches (20 to 38 millimetres), with the shorter distance ideal. The bobbin should be held in the hand at all times while you are applying thread to the dressing. With a little practice you can achieve tension control by putting pressure on the thread spool with your third finger.

Using the Whipfinisher

The whipfinisher is a simple tool to operate once its mechanical operation is understood. Many students take several evenings to master it, and when they have they are mystified why it was initially so difficult.

Whipfinishers are not, however, adapted to left-handed tying. The solution is for a left-handed person to work the thread clockwise (when looking from the eye towards the bend). If all operations are done in this manner, a whipfinisher can be used by a left-handed tyer.

Follow closely the whipfinisher diagrams on the next four pages. With a little practice on a bare hook, mastery of this tool is quite simple. The following are some problems that may arise.

If, when the pigtail end is disengaged, the thread pulls off the head of the fly, it is because the tool was not previously returned to a position at right angles to the hook.

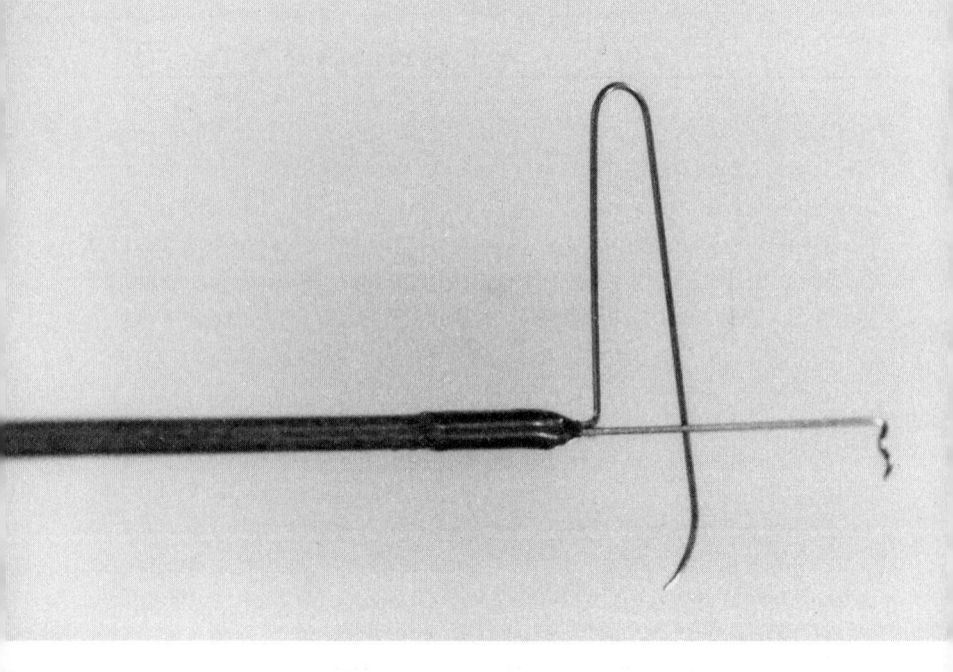

Using the Whipfinisher

With spring (A) down and thread (B) at right angles to hook (D) and whipfinisher (E) parallel with hook shank (D), engage thread (B) with hook (C), then swing both at the same time as indicated by arrows.

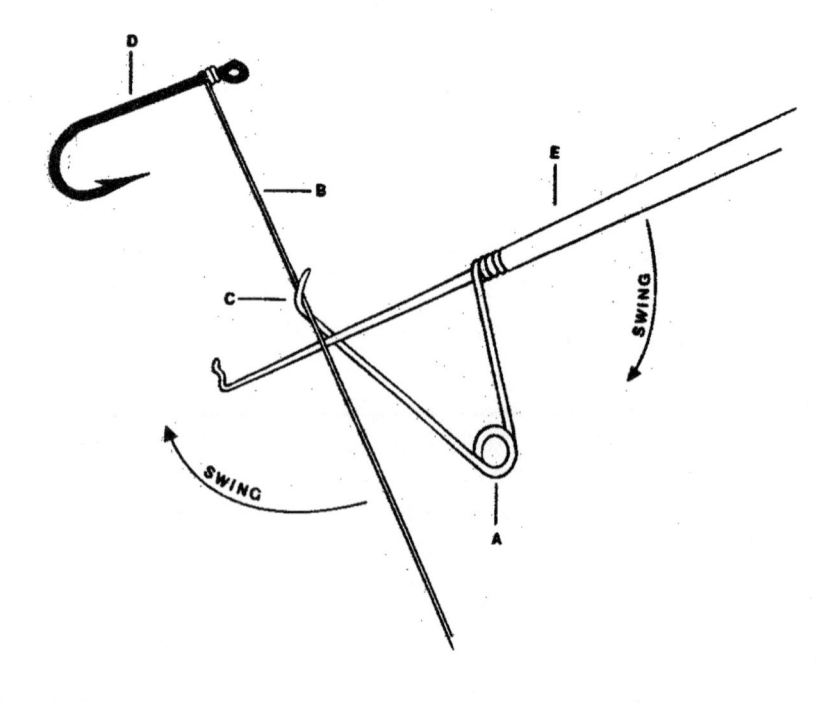

Problems of a Novice Fly Tyer 57

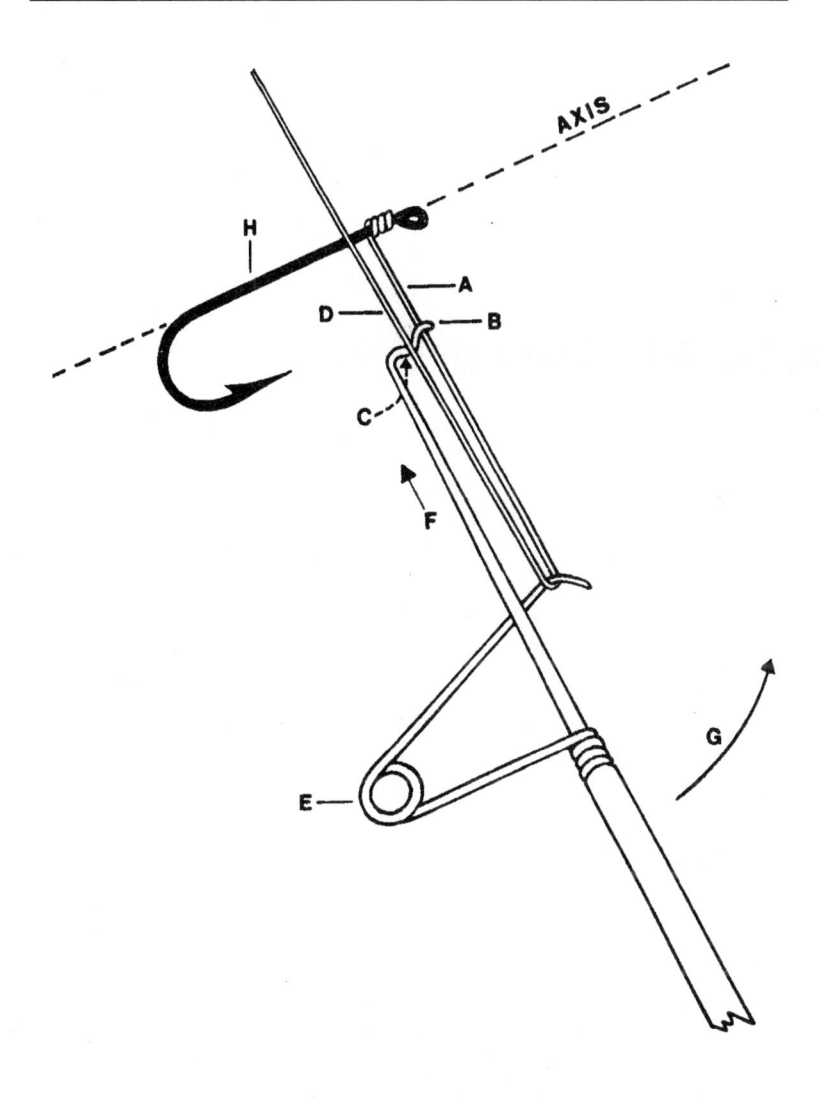

With the whipfinisher spring hook (E) down, engage thread (A) with hook (B). With a half turn clockwise, hook (C) should engage thread (D). In the position it should now be in, with (E) up, move whipfinish tool in the direction (F) until (C) is against hook (H). Now swing tool in the direction indicated by (G) until it is on the same axis as (H).

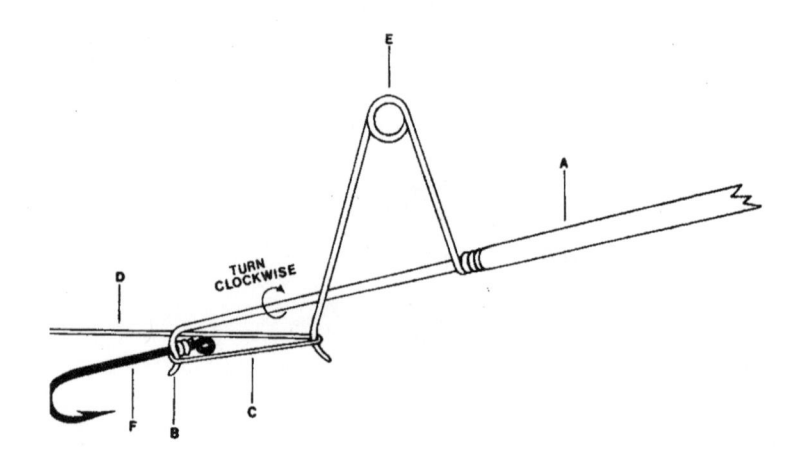

As whipfinisher tool (A) is turned clockwise, hook (B) carries the thread (C) over thread (D). Make three or four turns, stopping with (E) up, then return tool to a position at right angles to hook shank (F). (Enlarged drawing below).

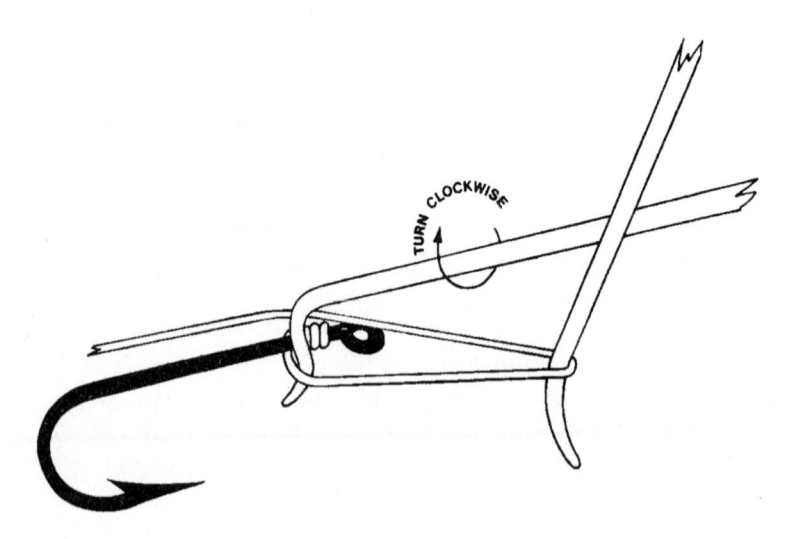

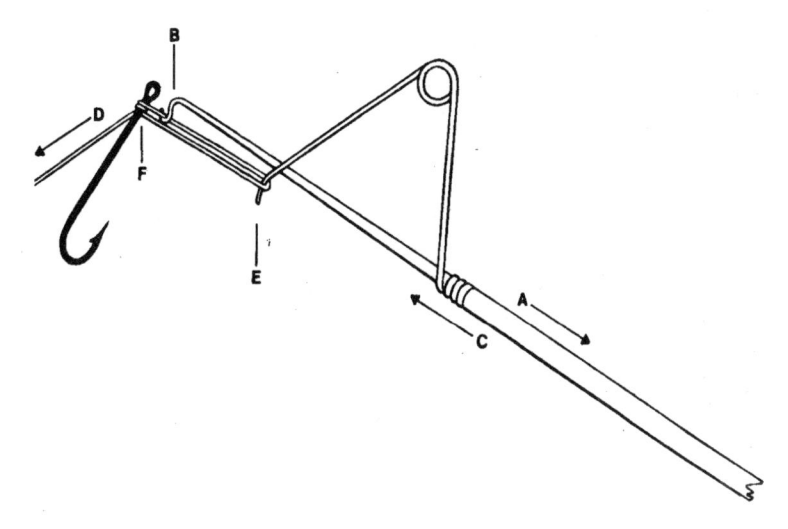

To disengage and complete knot, pull the tool back as (A) and lift (B). Then let the tool move forward (C), pulling on thread (D), unhooking (E) as it comes against hook shank at (F). Trim off loose end (D) close to knot and apply head cement to complete knot.

Should the thread slip off the spring hook prematurely, the thread was undoubtedly under too much tension during the winding operation.

Another potential difficulty is that the whipfinisher cannot be released even though the tool is at right angles to the hook. The problem is that while the tool is at right angles, the spring is pointing down, putting the pigtail on the far side of the hook where it cannot be drawn back to release it. The spring should be pointing up, with the tool at right angles to the hook. If the thread tension is not too tight it should now release easily. Unhook the pigtail, then pull the thread through with the bobbin on the far side. Keep the thread looped around the spring hook until it is drawn up to the head, then unhook and pull tight. All that remains is to put a drop of cement on the finished head and the fly is complete.

Finishing the Head Without a Whipfinishing Tool

Left-hand tyers who cannot use a whipfinisher and find it difficult to whipfinish by hand often have to revert to half hitches. So do some right-handers. Three half hitches will do an efficient job, either tied by hand or with the help of a ballpoint pen with retractable filler (described below). You can, however, create a true whipfinish without using the whipfinishing tool. The following instructions, practised on a bare hook using a good strong thread, will enable left-handers to master hand-finishing the fly. (Right-handers who dislike whipfinishing tools can substitute right hand for left.) The result is exactly the same as with a whipfinisher.

Pull about 4 to 6 inches (10 to 15 centimetres) of thread off the bobbin with the end fastened immediately behind the eye of the hook you are about to practise on. Holding the bobbin in your right hand, place the first and second finger of the left hand on top of the thread. Then take the bobbin over the far side of the second finger, turn your wrist towards you and roll the fingers over so the index finger is uppermost. The thread should now be crossed. With the second finger move the thread towards you. At the same time move the thread from the index finger over the hook. Now move the tip of the bobbin tube close to the hook, and by rolling (turning) the fingers inside the loop of thread, wrap the thread off the first finger around the head three or four times. Place your thumb on the eye to keep the wraps from pulling off. By moving the bobbin, disengage your fingers as you pull the thread tight. Cut off the thread and lacquer the head.

Half Hitch With a Pen

While it is not difficult to tie half hitches by hand, it is even easier with a simple tool. Although there are special tools available commercially, they are difficult to locate because there is little demand. The answer is a ballpoint pen with the tube removed. The pens are readily available at little cost and are as efficient as the factory tool.

To use the pen, pull thread from the bobbin toward you. With about 1 to 2 inches (4 to 5 centimetres) of thread between the bobbin and the hook eye, lay the open end of the pen on top of the thread and parallel to the axis of the hook shank. Take one turn of thread over the pen, place the open end over the eye, and slide the thread on to the hook. The result? One half hitch. Repeat three times, use lacquer or head cement on the head, cut off the thread, and the head is tied off.

Note that when using half hitches, you lacquer before cutting the thread. Should the half hitches not be well cemented, the last half hitch can come undone, leaving a tag of thread hanging loose from the head. Often unnoticed, this tag to some degree spoils the fly's efficiency.

I have found, incidentally, that I can take two wraps over the pen and slide them off in the same manner. If these wraps are done at the last, losing the last half hitch is less common.

PART TWO

THE POINT OF THE GAME

As it is for the loon, catching trout is the fly fisher's aim. Unlike the loon, however, we must convince trout our imitation flies are the real thing, and the real thing trout happen to want at any given moment. That is no easy task.

Chapter 8

Impression and Imitation

The starting point for fooling trout is to examine the foods they feed upon. Simple observation can tell you a lot, but you really do need to look at the fine details of whatever food item trout might prefer. Catching insects and other invertebrates is therefore vital. You will often find specimens in the gullets of captured trout, but you can greatly expand your knowledge by catching living creatures. Sometimes this is easy, but usually it takes some effort. A small aquarium net mounted on the tip section of an old fly rod is invaluable for this work. It can be extended with the butt section if required, and it takes up little room in a small boat.

Once you've had a good look at a favoured trout food, though, keep in mind that you cannot create a similar insect or other invertebrate trout food. You can only create an impression of it. This impression is akin to a photograph that is out of focus. An attempt to tie a fly with such details as six legs complete with knee joints and feet, eyeballs, and antennae is, to say the least, ridiculous. Such exactness is not impression but an attempt to create an insect. Good advice for the beginner is "Keep it simple."

A good impression involves five factors: form, colour, texture, attitude, and movement. Form involves size, outline, number of appendages, and appendage length.

Colour is self-explanatory, except that you absolutely must examine the food form in the water, since colour changes dramatically in the air.

Texture is mostly appearance. Food items that have a dark, opaque exoskeleton appear hard, while a translucent body is soft, or appears to be. Some insects have what seems to be body hair, which also gives the impression of softness.

Attitude refers to the food form's location in the water—whether it is at or near the surface, mid-water, or bottom, and whether it is in a vertical or horizontal position.

Movement is accomplished in a variety of ways. Each order has its own method. As well, as insects develop through larvae, pupae/nymph, and terrestrial stages, their method of movement reflects the stage of development. Invertebrates such as shrimp and leech, while they have no terrestrial stage, vary similarly. Many aquatic invertebrates remain motionless for long periods, or crawl laboriously along the bottom. At other times, some emit a jet of water from the rectal orifice and move rapidly. Some are accomplished swimmers, travelling at good speed over long distances. A worm-like body undulation is a method used by many organisms, large and small. Other creatures, usually air breathers, float to the surface where they trap a bubble of air on their body, then swim rapidly to the bottom.

To create the impression of an insect with an artificial fly, the first thing to consider is size and dimension. Then select the proper hook for body length—2X, 3X, 4X long, etc.—and the size of gape for body breadth—6, 8, 10, etc. (See the chapter on hooks.) The style of hook is your choice.

Material selection is very important and should not be done with a "This is close enough" attitude for size, texture, modelling, or colour. Soft-bodied flies usually require fur or hair applied as a dubbing, or chenille. Firm or hard bodies make good use of wool yarns, cotton, floss, raffia, and similar materials. When selecting material for the body, think about how the material will behave underwater.

Soft body material can give an impression of life by means of the alternately slimming and swelling action as the fly is drawn through the water with a pull-and-pause retrieve. A hard body will reflect light to some extent, giving the illusion of the hard exoskeleton of aquatic insects. A soft, palmered hackle also imparts a breathing, lifelike appearance, while a stiff hackle does not. The stiff hackle is therefore inappropriate for many imitations, but it can be just right for imitating the small bits of stick and weed that sedge cases are made of.

Consider a material's buoyancy. Large dry flies are best dressed with as light a material as possible. So much the better if the dressing resists water absorption. This means it will float longer without frequent applications of fly dressing.

The hackle used to represent legs can be spotted, mottled, barred, or a solid colour. Hackle feathers, quills, hair, and even rubber can be used. Since long flies require long hackle to realistically represent legs, their hackle must therefore be stiffer than the ordinary roosterneck hackle. Flue from the side of a quill is more suitable and frequently has a better range of modelling characteristics. Hair has a similar advantage. On any fly, too soft a hackle will mat or become floppy. It should be soft enough to give the illusion of life, yet stiff enough to stay in the proper position. On large flies, the thickness of hackle fibres also should be considered. A large dragonfly nymph, for instance, has thicker, longer legs than a tiny mayfly nymph. Material must be selected with this difference in mind.

The wing case on many nymphs requires close attention. On some nymphs, wing-case colour changes as the insects approach emergence. The cases also become larger and more robust. For this reason, as emergence time approaches, artificials should have more material on the wing case and it should be a darker colour.

Inexperienced fly tyers often shrug off body ribbing as unimportant, something just there to attract attention. This attitude is wrong. Careful selection of material is required if it is to adequately fulfil its purpose. If it has no purpose, eliminate it.

The body of most insects is segmented. If the insect has a hard exoskeleton, it reflects light off certain angles or portions of each segment. Colour of the reflected light depends on many factors: suspended matter in the water, time of day and of year, whether the day is sunny or cloudy. Good fly fishers know that light quality is rarely consistent for more than a few minutes from daylight to dark. Light is continually changing, not only during the day but also from week to week and month to month. To have a separate fly for each light condition obviously would require an astronomical number of flies. For this reason there are a few rules that adequately serve, although they are a guide only and there is ample latitude for innovation. On bright days use silver ribbing; on dull days and in spring and fall, use gold ribbing. On hard or smooth bodies use silver or gold tinsel. On soft or furry flies use white, yellow, or black thread.

For ribbing material, cotton thread is much better than nylon. Cotton remains opaque in water while nylon goes translucent. To a great extent, nylon takes on whatever body colour it ribs, defeating the purpose of the ribbing. To imitate some insects that carry air bubbles from which they breathe while under water, silver tinsel reflects light about the same way the air bubble does. If the tinsel is overlaid with plastic, the effect is even more authentic.

These bubble-carrying insects are often species of beetle, and most carry the small bubble on the tip of their abdomen. As I said earlier, photosynthesis that takes place in water weeds in bright sunshine produces oxygen that appears as strings of tiny bubbles rising to the surface. Many insects moving through these strings of bubbles gather them on their bodies, where they appear as minute silver balls. When tinsel is used to imitate bubbles, it's best to partly bury the tinsel in the body material so there is just a glint here and there. The appearance is then natural and effective.

Is this natural look important? Well, how often have you caught a fish on the first cast or two, then nothing until the fly was changed? With the new fly, the same thing happens until the fly is again changed. The problem is that the fish has mouthed the fly and destroyed the air bubbles trapped in the dry body fibres. It no longer appears natural.

Wings are a part of the terrestrial stage of every aquatic insect. Most mate in the terrestrial stage, lay their eggs in or on the water, and die there. Eggs are generally deposited on the water surface, but a number of insect species in the order Trichoptera (sedgeflies) and Odonata (dragonflies and damselflies) fold their wings and swim to the bottom. Here they deposit their eggs, then endeavour to reach the surface. Being now physically spent, few reach the surface alive.

Dry-fly wings are made from a wide variety of materials. Hair and feathers are standard, but various synthetic materials are now widely used. Dry-fly wings are generally tied in an upright position and slightly divided, a method that looks natural for mayflies and, to a lesser extent, newly emerged sedges. A practical aspect is that the wings act as a rudder when the fly is dropping to the water, assuring that it will land with its wings up. Observant anglers know, however, that dry-fly wings should be affixed in whatever way best imitates the insect you're trying to represent.

The wet fly, also called a "down wing," uses the same wide variety of materials for wings. However, the material selected is to some degree more critical than for the dry fly. As already mentioned, for a fly dressed with quill segments it is imperative that the segments be taken from the leading edges of a left-hand feather and a right-hand feather to form a matched pair. If both sections are from a right-hand or a left-hand feather, the identical curve will make the fly spin as it is drawn through the water. (A right-hand feather means a quill from the right wing; a left-hand, from the left wing.) The

*A newly emerged Gomphus dragonfly
and empty cases on a birch tree.*

leading edge of a feather should always be used. The trailing edge is much softer and frequently has a reverse curve, making it difficult to work with and less durable. In many cases the "wing" is intended to resemble the back of a wingless pupa or nymph and should therefore be of a soft texture that blends in with the body.

Many fly dressers have an affliction that could be called a "tail" complex. It seems that every fly they tie is decorated with a tail, whether the insect being represented has a tail or not. Let's be practical. If an insect has a tail or something that looks like a tail, then put one on. If not, you'd best have a good reason for the unnatural addition.

Some beetle larvae (order Coleoptera) have short tails of what appear to be two forked hairs. They are short in comparison to the length of the body and are usually drab in colour. Mayfly and damselfly nymphs also have tails. The tails on mayfly nymphs are usually three setae, equal to the body in length, while damselfly nymphs have three broad, paddle-like appendages not unlike the tail surfaces on an aircraft. Freshwater shrimp seem to have a short tail the same colour as the body. Chironomids often have a pupal-sac remnant that looks like a tail. Dragonfly nymphs have posterior spines that also seem like a tail. Other than those mentioned, I can think of no other subsurface insect imitation that justifies any kind of tail. Leech imitations, minnow imitations, and general attractor flies are another matter, as are thick "tails" intended to simulate insect bodies, but the often gaudy appendages found on too many wet-fly patterns are counterproductive.

The dry fly, on the other hand, has a good reason for being dressed with a tail. Not the gaudy reds and yellows on commercial dressings, but reasonable attachments that look natural. A properly tied tail on a dry fly supports it in a natural attitude on the water, keeping the rear of the hook up and helping to maintain the fly in a level position. That alone can justify adding a tail (even if the natural lacks one), but a tail can also simulate the shell case attached to an insect during its transition from pupae to terrestrial.

Be it a mayfly, midge, sedge, or any other insect that emerges in open water (as opposed to the orders that clamber up sticks, rushes, trees, and logs), when it reaches the surface the wing case splits and the new terrestrial clambers out. It then sits momentarily, wings upright to dry, on the forward end of the now empty pupal or nymphal case. The empty case, from below, looks like a tail. I recommend that an angler gather a few empty cases, float them on a glass of water, and look at them from underneath to assess colour, length, and volume. This exercise helps you to judge how best to simulate the empty case in the form of a tail.

A phrase frequently heard wherever fly fishermen gather is "standard patterns." For the most part, however, patterns aren't standard. Quite the contrary. Although tyers may dress flies to supposedly standard formulae, they vary them as whim, material, and creativity dictate. They are also relying on what someone else told them was the "true" pattern. That "someone else" might be quite wrong. When you are told that a given pattern is "the fly to use," it is always a good idea to look at the actual pattern your informant is using. It might be very different from your notions of that pattern. It might be that it works only because it is just a little like the real thing. Standard flies are, after all, standards because they work in a wide range of areas and situations. Tying a fly that better imitates whatever food item trout prefer on any given day will generally produce better results. It's been my observation that anglers relying on Grizzly Kings, Black Gnats, and such suffer much frustration when fishing beside an angler who is knowledgeable about local trout foods, ties flies to imitate those foods, and then presents them properly.

When you become familiar with trout foods, it will soon become apparent that the so-called standard patterns have many more faults than virtues. That realization may prompt you to take up fly tying, but even if you are indisposed to make that step, you can often alter standard patterns enough to make them far more effective. If you know what the real thing looks like, a pair of sharply pointed scissors, used with care, can change a useless fly into a reasonable producer. It's also possible now to buy excellent imitations from specialty fly shops. You still must know, however, just what is required on any given day. Gaining knowledge of trout foods is definitely the best route to less frustration and more fish.

Chapter 9

A Detective Story

Coming up with the right fly involves detective work not unlike that of Sherlock Holmes. In most cases, your clues come only from the fish and the creatures on which they feed. Sometimes, though, other anglers and their preferred flies must be added to your pondering.

The case of the immature damselfly comes to mind here.

It all began when Bob Allen and Heber Smith (two late friends) were gathered with me in my fly-tying room. We were all having a "wee drap of Scottish dew," and Bob was describing a recent fishing trip and the fly that had been absolutely deadly. He showed us the fly, but Heber and I weren't much impressed by it. It had an orangish yellow wool body on a #8 standard hook with a mallard flank feather rolled and tied over the top. The feather extended beyond the bend of the hook about the length of the hook. That was it. No ribbing, hackle, or tail.

We believed Bob, though, when he reported two days of fast fishing for trout in the two- to four-pound class. He said he had only to cast that fly (but only that fly) out on a dry line towards the sedge grass and then retrieve it slowly and erratically. The strikes were hard and solid.

Bob gave me a sample of the pattern, but I just filed it away in a collection of flies given me over the years. I never used or copied it. Instead, I began a thought process aimed at discovering just why that fly had worked so well. Once I understood that, I reasoned, I could make up an even better pattern—or at least know why the silly thing worked at all.

The first clue in the "chain of evidence" was the time of year. Bob had been fishing in mid-July, and that is not really an active feeding time for the trout in the lake Bob fished. An examination of stomach contents generally reveals a dramatically shrunken stomach and little more than odd, varied food items. You might find blood worms, chironomids, shrimp, water boatman, damselfly nymphs, or various forms of zooplankton and similarly tiny insect larvae. Larger fish might also contain a small leech. No sedge, mayfly, or dragonfly though, in any stage—not in that lake at that time.

I considered all those possibilities and then examined the anonymous fly. Clearly it was too large to be imitating the smaller food forms. The short, robust body made me think of water boatman, but it was too early for the fall emergence and too late for the spring emergence of that insect. Trout would not feed selectively on what few offbeat water boatman might be available. Anyway, the resemblance to a water boatman was pretty vague.

Resemblance to blood worms, shrimp, or chironomid pupae was even vaguer, and the way Bob fished the fly made them even easier to dismiss. Blood worms and shrimp would be found near bottom and Bob's fly had to be working near the surface. His retrieve was probably too fast to imitate a chironomid pupa, and anyway, the strike to chironomid imitations is seldom of the dramatic sort Bob had experienced.

That left only damselfly nymphs, but this really didn't make sense. The early instars of those insects would be in deeper water and too well hidden to create selective feeding. Nymphs moving shoreward to emerge would roughly resemble the anonymous fly, but it was a bit late for that migration, and trout feeding on those insects generally want a better imitation than Bob's fly provided.

Puzzling.

But then I added another possibility to the list: immature damselflies in terrestrial form

Damselflies, after clambering ashore after their migration, climb a stem of sedge grass or other convenient object until they reach an obstacle. Under no circumstances will they backtrack. Once stopped, they find a firm foothold and eventually begin their emergence.

The skin splits open across the head around the level of the eyes, and the insect forces its head through the split to crack the rest of the skin lengthwise down the wing case. Pulling its legs free, the insect then draws its long body out, arching it high in the air to escape the nymphal case. The wings start to unfold then, and the body grows lengthwise. For several minutes the body and wings take turns in this "stretching exercise." In about a half hour the insect will have the typical blue colour and the form of the terrestrial damselfly—but until then it is typically a pale Naples yellow colour (a light greenish yellow) and shaped quite a lot like Bob's anonymous fly (which was, you'll recall, yellow in colour).

Bob had mentioned there were frequent gusts of wind during his trip, and that clinched the case. Immature damselflies must have been blown into the water in good numbers—helpless and succulent enough to draw even mid-July's lethargic trout.

I naturally tied up a more realistic version of Bob's fly, which has proven very effective whenever the right conditions occur. My fly features an extended body formed on 40-pound-test monofilament. The body is of dyed yellow seal fur dubbing ribbed with gold or silver tinsel. The wing case is a mallard flank feather dyed a light yellowish tan. A Naples yellow hackle is palmered over the thorax and topped with the wing case. Spent polar bear hair wings are tied in behind the thorax, and eyes are formed by burning the tips of a short length of monofilament affixed at the head. It's a complex fly, but it really does seem to work well—both dry and submerged.

The point I want to make here, though, is that it will work only when conditions are right. And only a knowledge of trout and trout foods can tell you when conditions are right. Keep in mind, too, that should you find conditions like those Bob encountered (and recognize them), you might fare just fine with a simple fly that only roughly mimics the real insect. You'll certainly fare better than you would with a perfect imitation of an insect trout just aren't interested in.

Check It

If you hear a click when casting, check your fly. It may have hit the boat. This contact frequently breaks the point off at the barb, and you will not likely notice the break until a number of fish have been lost.

Leaky Boat?

For minor leaks—and even some major ones—carry a tube of Silicone Sealer in your tackle box. Should your boat develop a leak, dry the area and apply the sealer. The boat can be used in well under half an hour. The Sealer also works well on small cracks and holes.

Noisy Oar Locks

Rub the male part with candle wax or with the dressing for your floating line. It is dry, not messy, and an efficient lubricant.

PART THREE

FLY TYING FOR EVERYONE

Chapter 10

Making the Flies

Woolly Worm (Sedgefly Larva)

Order—Trichoptera (See page 129.)
The fly known as the Woolly Worm is an old commercial pattern, tied in a large number of colours and sizes. This pattern is the basis of many artificial flies and is used to dress imitations of some sedgefly larvae, better known as cased caddis. Variations of colour and material can be used as necessary. Popular dry flies known as Variants and Bi-visibles are dressed using the same mechanical operations.

The cased caddis is the larval stage of the sedgefly. It is a worm-like organism that builds a case out of weeds and plants among which it lives. Most species of caddis build portable cases in which they clumsily clamber about the bottom weed growth, feeding on both plant and animal life. Each species has its own case design. Since authorities claim there are over 750 species in the order Trichoptera in North America, it is impractical to even attempt to address them all. The one we are interested in is the larva of the large traveller sedgefly.

The larval case is usually about 1 inch (26 millimetres) long by 1/4 inch (7 millimetres) in diameter. It is generally made of chara weed, cut in short pieces and laid spirally in shingle fashion parallel to the central axis of the case, the forward end being the larger. It is also common to find cases made from bits of bottom debris or other material.

With few exceptions the larva will be attached in a lengthwise position in the case. The larva grasps the case with a pair of hooks on the rear of its body as it moves about the bottom vegetation. The worm inside the well-camouflaged case is a pale bluish green with whitish hair-like gills on either side of the body. Constant undulations of its body move water through the case and over the gills, supplying oxygen. The six legs are an orange tan, and its head is the same colour with dark stripes running lengthwise.

At pupation time the case is fastened to a branch of vegetation or something similar. The larva constructs a grillwork of bottom weed or debris, sealing itself inside where the transformation into a pupa takes place.

With an understanding of the foregoing information, you can easily tie an effective imitation, which also provides a good introduction to fly tying. After tying a few good Woolly Worms, you'll be ready to move along to more complex patterns and will also have some very effective flies.

Materials required are:

Hook: #6 or 8 Mustad 9672, 3X long, forged, tapered-down eye

Thread: Medium brown, waxed 6/0

Tail: Large brown hackle feather

Ribbing: Fine oval gold (optional)

Body: Olive green and/or olive brown chenille

Hackle: Rooster-neck hackle

With the hook in the vise, put a coat of head cement on the shank and start the thread just behind the eye. Then, using 10 or so quick turns, wrap the thread to where the shank starts to dip into the bend. Let the bobbin hang and take approximately 5/8 inch (16 millimetres) of flue off the side of a large brown hackle feather. Gather it into a bunch and with your right hand place it on top of the hook at the bend in position for a tail. Length, from the extreme rear of the hook, should be no longer than the depth of the bite. Without moving the tail material, change hands and tie down the tail with three or four turns of thread. (Should you have difficulty, review the section on making the tail in "Problems of a Novice Fly Tyer" on page 52.)

After spreading the flue to a position at right angles to the quill, tie in a large hackle feather by the tip, the outside of the feather facing you.

Prepare a length of medium-size chenille, olive green or olive brown, by removing about 3/16 inch (5 millimetres) of fluff from the end so that just the bare thread shows. While the end you choose is your preference, you will notice, if you pull the strand back and forth through your fingers, that there is a definite grain in the way it is set in the threads. The chenille is tied only by the thread where the tail and hackle feathers are tied down—this method prevents bulking at the end of the body. When all is secure, run the thread quickly, in open turns, to 3/16 inch (2 millimetres) from the eye.

In tight turns now wrap the chenille up to the end and fasten it with three or four firm turns of thread. Cut off the excess chenille, and with a few additional turns wrap down any loose ends. Let the bobbin hang. Now we come to "palmering" a hackle feather. With hackle pliers, grasp the butt end of the hackle and, keeping it on edge, with firm pressure wrap it in several evenly spaced turns to a position immediately behind the eye. Put a drop of head cement on the end. Then, with a number of turns of thread, build up a neat head. Tie the head off with the whipfinisher, cut off the remaining thread, apply head cement, and the fly is finished. If you wish to shorten the hackle, you can trim it to the desired length with careful use of scissors.

By using two contrasting colours of similar size chenille, you can make a body with either rings or stripes. Twist the two colours together, then carefully wrap the chenille on the hook, creating a two-tone effect. Twist the strands together clockwise to produce rings; twist them anti-clockwise for stripes.

Should you wish to have a tinsel rib, tie it in at the bend of the hook, after the chenille but before the hackle. The chenille should be wrapped clockwise but tinsel, in order to stand out well, should be applied counter-clockwise so that it doesn't get lost between the turns of chenille. When done as suggested it crosses the turns and isn't lost. The hackle should follow in a clockwise manner.

Blood Worm

Order—Diptera, Family—Chironomus (See page 130.)
Chironomids are one of the most abundant of aquatic insects and the major item in a trout's diet during much of the season. Unlike many insects, they are a valuable fish food at all stages of development.

The blood worm is the larval stage of the chironomid fly, a large family of insects with over 1000 members. They can be as small as a few millimetres to over 1 inch (nearly 26 millimetres) long, and from thread-like to slightly under 1/16 inch (2 millimetres) in diameter. Colours range from pale watery green to medium green and red through a rather dark maroon. The larvae I have most commonly found in fish are 3/8 to 9/16 inches (10 to 15 millimetres), long and deep red or maroon.

In this larval stage they inhabit the lake bottom, living in tubes they build vertically in the mud or marl. Some species live in gelatinous tubes built on the bottom weeds, pupating in them and leaving when the pupae are fully developed. I have seen them free swimming, so at some time during the larval stage they must feel the urge to travel, for what reason I do not know.

To represent this insect in an artificial, material selection is important, especially when dressing a new pattern. Hooks are the first consideration because they are the foundation of the dressing and the basis of the fly. A hook that straightens under pressure is useless, so most, if not all, hooks made with round wire are inappropriate. As already mentioned, a forged hook is flat on either side, much like a floor joist in a house, which provides greatly increased strength over one made with round wire. A forged hook is the obvious choice.

Another consideration is the depth of bite required (the "gape"). As gape size increases, the wire gets thicker and heavier. Since the blood worm pattern we are about to tie has a thin body, we want to retain thin wire. Fortunately, the gape need not be deep, and we can fare well with a hook that has a long shank and a modest gape. A satisfactory hook for our purpose needs a shank about 9/16 inch (15 millimetres) long and a gape of 3/16 inch (5 millimetres). A #12 model 79580 T.D. (turned down) tap (tapered) eye meets these requirements. (The 12 is the depth of gape and 79580 is the shank length, in this case 4X long. These numbers apply to Mustad Viking hooks, which are my preference.)

To represent the rear end of the insect's body, frequently quite dark owing to the food in the digestive tract, we will use several strands of black bear hair, with fine copper wire imitating the segmentation. The body, a medium to dark maroon, requires a durable material with a rather solid finish to reasonably imitate the insect's chitinous outer structure. Wool serves admirably. Carefully applied, it will have a smooth enough surface, and when it's roughed up a bit by a few fish, it will acquire a slight translucence, giving the fly a more natural appearance.

Although hackle is usually put on a fly to represent wings or legs, another use is to create the impression of movement. It should be selected with care, since texture is very important. If it is too soft it will simply mat and cling to the body; if too stiff there will be no movement at all. The colour should not contrast with the body but must be similar in colour and tone if possible. Use only a few strands. We are not trying to add to the body's dimension but rather to provide something that will move a bit to give the impression of life. Hackle should be no longer than the body, distributed evenly around it, and close but not tight. It must be free to show some movement.

For the head I use black thread. I've most often found this particular blood worm in black muck, and I believe that is why its head is nearly black.

Hook: #12 Mustad 79580, 4X long, turned down, tapered eye
Thread: Black 6.0
Tail: Black bear hair
Ribbing: Fine copper wire
Body: Medium to dark maroon tapestry wool
Hackle: Cock pheasant saddle (red phase)

Start tying this fly by putting the hook in the vise. Clamp it with the barb just clear of the vise jaw, eye slightly higher than the bend end of the shank. An angle of 15 degrees is about right to keep the thread from slipping off the head when the bobbin is left hanging.

Tie in as a tail a dozen hairs, more or less, no longer than the depth of the bite. Then tie in a strand of copper wire about 4 1/2 inches (12 centimetres) long and as thick as an ordinary sewing thread. When the tail and wire are secure, run the thread in several spaced turns to a position about 3/16 inch (5 millimetres) from the eye.

Cut a 5-inch (13-centimetre) length from a hank of dark maroon tapestry wool and divide it into single strands. Take a single strand, and with the long end extending past the bend, tie the other end where the thread hangs with three or four tight turns. Now move the thread to within 1/16 inch (2 millimetres) of the eye and let the bobbin hang. With hackle pliers grasp the wool about 1 1/2 inches (4 centimetres) from the hook and start to wrap it around the shank. When the wool gets too short between the hackle pliers and the shank, take a new hold but do not exceed the 1 1/2 inch (4 centimetres) length. If you do, the wool will part.

When the wraps of thread that hold the tail and ribbing in place are covered (just where the shank starts to dip into the bend), return the wool to the eye in the same manner. Just before reaching the thread, with finger and thumb turn the wool on the shank to be sure it is tight. You may have to take another turn or two to bring the wool into position at the thread to tie it off. Cut the remaining wool off and keep it for the next fly. Then take a few additional turns of thread to tie any loose fibres of the cut end.

With hackle pliers hold the copper wire as you did the wool and wrap it in seven evenly spaced turns in the opposite rotation to the wool. With this method it will not be lost in the wool, as it will cross the wraps. Take two turns of thread over the wire, then bend it back on itself, tie it down, and cut off excess wire. It is now locked in and cannot pull loose.

For the hackle, use a long, dark reddish-brown feather from the rump of a cock Chinese pheasant. Clean any fluff and soft flue from the base, then, holding the feather by the tip, pull the flue gently down until the ends are even. Hold several strands firmly and strip from the quill by pulling them towards the butt. Hold the butts in the right hand and place them on the far side of the hook so the tips are even with the end of the body, then change hands. Now, holding the butt in place with the left hand, take two or three turns of thread over it. The outside of the feather should face to the outside.

Repeat the operation as before, but place the feather on the side closest to you, again with the outside of the feather to the outside. Two turns of thread will hold it. Then with finger and thumb, twist the butts back and forth around the hook until the flue is evenly distributed. Wrap down with a few more tight turns of thread. With your left hand holding the hackle in place, add more turns, easing pressure as you work towards the bend. After about four turns, move to the eye again, gradually increasing pressure. Form a nice head, then whip off the thread, cut it loose, add a drop of head cement, and the fly is ready for your favourite lake.

The hackle should lie close but not tight to the body. If it does not lie close and is inclined to flare, it is probably because the body has been wrapped up to the eye, making a blunt end rather than a nice taper. This will block the feather close to a right angle. Another reason for flare could be that when the thread was run back on the final wraps, it was done too tightly.

Leech

Order—Hirudinea (See page 131.)
Lakes and ponds in most areas of the world are home to the many members of the leech family. Although the leech is a far more important food for trout than is commonly believed, fish seem to be very particular about size. While it is not uncommon to see leeches 4 to 6 inches (10 to 15 centimetres) long, they are usually about 2 to 4 inches (5 to 10 centimetres). Trout appear to favour those from 1 1/2 to 2 3/4 inches (4 to 7 centimetres). Rarely, even in large fish, have I found specimens over 3 1/2 inches (9 centimetres).

The common colours on which the fish feed are black, brown mottled with darker blotches of no particular pattern, and a rusty maroon, the result of a blood meal in the digestive system.

While the leech's food is widely varied, the primary source, at least from my observation, is snails. I have, however, watched them feeding on shrimp, blood worms, and many dead and dying organisms. They attach themselves to turtles and frogs when the opportunity arises, as well as human beings.

The leech is soft and rubbery to the touch, its body wrinkled, lined, and segmented. None of these characteristics, though, are well defined to the casual observer. The posterior is flattened laterally and rounded at the extremity, then it tapers and becomes round towards the anterior end, where it is bluntly pointed. It is equipped with a suction device at either end (a small disc at the front and a large one at the rear).

A leech moves slowly about the bottom by fastening its forward end to some object, then bringing its rear end to the forward position through body contraction and looping. It then releases the forward end, which waves around searching for a new place to take hold. When one is found it repeats the procedure. At other times it will swim close to the bottom with an undulating movement, body fully extended. Much less frequently it swims vertically just under the surface, body fully extended and lazily undulating with little or no apparent forward progress.

Technically speaking, a leech representation cannot be called a fly. But it seems to me equally erroneous to refer to it as a lure. I will, therefore, take advantage of the broad definition of a fly in Webster's *New World Dictionary* and unashamedly refer to the leech as a fly.

Any fly fisher who does not have a good leech pattern is missing some fine sport. Unfortunately, while there are a variety of good patterns, they are seldom commercially available in any but specialty fly shops.

The following pattern can be successfully tied in several colours and in almost any size. Keep in mind, however, that the larger the fly, the greater the difficulty in casting. And as already mentioned, trout do not particularly like very large leeches. Their preference, it seems, is for a fly about 1 1/2 inches (4 to 5 centimetres) long and not too bulky.

The following materials are required to dress a pattern that I have used with great success for many years:

Hook: #8 Mustad 9672, 3X long. Also practical are #10-9672 or 79580, 4X long

Thread: Black, waxed 6/0 (Danville's Fly Master waxed thread is very good, not only for this pattern but also for practically any other.)

Tail: The tail end requires a fairly stiff hair because it must maintain a broad expanded appearance when wet in order to well represent the leech's wide, flat posterior. Seal fur is the ideal material, but since it's rarely available, in this particular pattern the under fur of black or polar bear, or calf tail (kip) dyed a jet black are satisfactory substitutes.

Ribbing: Gold, silver, or copper tinsel. It should be quite fine, well spaced, and fairly well buried in the body material. It is not intended to represent body segments but to reflect light, imitating the smooth body of the natural insect and possibly adding an element of attraction.

Mid-body: Black mohair. For the mid-body, a finer, softer hair with a little spring to it when in the water imparts the impression of life. This impression is an important consideration in many patterns. I have found mohair to be the ideal material. If it is not available from a wool shop, pure dyed mohair is usually available at some of the better fly-tying supply houses. It comes in hanks about 3/4 inch

(20 millimetres) round and approximately 8 inches (20 centimetres) long.

Front body: Black Angora wool. The front body section requires a material that has some tendency to mat so there won't be too much expansion. This matting allows the body to maintain a reasonably authentic shape without destroying the impression of life. Angora knitting wool serves very well, especially the fluffy kind.

To tie the leech, put the hook in the vise, lacquer the full length of the shank with head cement, and immediately start the thread behind the eye, taking it to the bend in spaced turns. Take a few extra turns, let the bobbin hang, and prepare the tail-end fur.

With a fairly good pinch of hair between finger and thumb of your left hand, place some of the ends on the shank at the bend and take two firm turns of thread over them. Then pull away as much hair as will come easily. Repeat as many times as necessary to build a good bushy tail about 5/8 inch (15 millimetres) long.

Over the wraps that hold the tail in place, tie in a 3- to 4-inch (7- to 10-centimetre) length of tinsel. Tie it in by the tip, the length extending over the eye, with two or three turns of thread. Then double it back so the length extends to the rear. Now take two more turns over the doubled end to securely lock it.

Should you be fortunate enough to have black, spun mohair wool, tie in a piece about 4 inches (10 centimetres) long. Draw all the fibres to a right angle from the central thread, then pull them to the rear as a turn is taken around the hook. Keep the turns close together and draw the fibres back with every turn to 5/16 inch (8 millimetres) from the eye. At this point drop three or four turns of thread over the end, cut off the remaining mohair, and let the bobbin hang. Now pull all the fibres back (a Velcro brush works well for this). If the fibres don't lie down, do not be concerned. We will solve the problem later.

If you cannot find prepared mohair wool, it may be necessary to use unspun mohair and make a dubbing. This kind of dubbing can be difficult to make because the long fibres must be largely at right angles to the main thread. If not done carefully it becomes rope-like, which is totally useless. Another way is to cut the hank of mohair into lengths about 1 1/2 inches (3 to 4 centimetres) long and apply it to the body in the same manner as the substitute seal fur was applied to the tail.

Caution: Apply only a small amount at a time and be sure it is even all around the hook.

Tie in a 3- to 4-inch (8- to 10-centimetre) length of the Angora wool 1/16 inch (2 millimetres) back onto the mohair and wrap it in a taper to the back of the eye. Tie it down and cut off the remainder. Then take a few extra turns and let the bobbin hang.

With hackle pliers take the tinsel, and with the dubbing needle lift the hair up, then wrap a turn of tinsel in the opposite direction to which the body was wrapped. As you continue to wrap the ribbing, keep lifting the hair so that it doesn't wrap down any mohair or Angora. At the eye drop two turns of thread over it, double it back, and put on three or four more turns. Form a small inconspicuous head, whipfinish it off, and put on a drop of head cement.

Now comb all the fibres back all the way around the body. A Velcro brush is excellent here. Do not forget to brush up the Angora wool. If necessary, pick it with the dubbing needle to raise a bit of a nap. In the water this nap will move slightly, adding to the life-like impression.

Take a pair of sharp scissors in your right hand, and with the left hand stroke and pull all the fibres to the extreme end of the tail. In a sliding, nibbly manner, scissor off the excessively long fibres so the end is blunt and somewhat rounded. Do not cut it square.

At this point the fly will be quite bushy and will not really look like a leech. But be patient. It is now time for the final treatment. With a pair of forceps, drop the fly into a container of very hot water for a few seconds, then grip it by the eye and move it up and down a few times to flow the hair together. Remove from the water, hold it to cool a few seconds, then use your fingers to stroke all the hair tightly together. Hook the fly into a piece of Styrofoam or some such material and let it dry. When it is thoroughly dry, trim off any wild hair fibres. The leech is ready for fishing.

Terrestrial Traveller Sedgefly

Order—Trichoptera (See page 132.)
When the emerging sedgefly breaks from the pupal case, it immediately raises its wings to a nearly vertical position to dry. At

this stage the wings are a pale green, but they quickly change colour, becoming a pale muddy brown mottled with darker markings. When the wings dry they are lowered to a tent-like position, and the sedgefly appears somewhat like a moth, an insect for which it is often mistaken, particularly by novice fly fishermen. The abdomen of the mature terrestrial is a dusty, medium sage green colour, while the thorax, legs, and head are a muddy cinnamon.

Since the wings are longer than the abdomen and held tent-like, they cover the sides of the body. For this reason it is not possible to see the abdomen as the fly skitters over the water prior to taking off for shoreline vegetation. The sedges fortunate enough to escape hungry fish and birds spend the afternoon in the trees and bushes along the shore where they copulate. In late afternoon and evening they fly out over the lake, again skittering, running, and dancing on the water, depositing their eggs to start another generation.

The traveller sedge is important to the fly fisher because it is one of the few major insects to provide seasonally consistent action for the dry-fly angler. For this reason a great many fly patterns have been designed to imitate this important terrestrial. Probably the most common and well known is the deer-hair pattern called the Tom Thumb. Over the years many fly tyers, including me, have tried to originate a better pattern, with varying degrees of success. I feel the pattern developed by Arthur Mitchaluk of Calgary, Alberta, is superior by far. Arthur is a serious and talented fly fisherman and tyer. The pattern he showed me years ago at Roche Lake has been a consistent producer whenever the big traveller sedges are active.

Hook: #10 Mustad 9672, 3X long

Thread: Although the pattern that was given to me was tied with black thread, I favour Danville's Fly Master waxed thread in a light to medium brown.

Tail and Wings: On Arthur's pattern these are made from elk body hair. But elk hair and I don't agree, so I use white-tail or mule deer buck hair, taken from the animal's back because it's darker than hair off the side.

Body: As near as I can tell from the pattern, the dubbing material is seal fur. Since seal fur is not often available, substitute one of the other many fine dubbing materials now available. Colour is a medium sage green that is slightly muddy, or "sad."

Hackle: The hackle is from a medium to dark red rooster cape, the feather about 1 to 2 inches (3 to 5 centimetres) long.

To tie the sedge, begin as usual with the hook in the vise at the required angle. Lacquer it with head cement, immediately start the thread, and in spaced turns run it to the bend of the hook.

Before starting to use the hair, clamp a plastic bag or an anti-static cloth (I use Bounce) to the tying bench in a convenient location. Then run your hands down it a few times to build up static electricity. Do this so that any hair sticking to your hands will be attracted to the bag, leaving them clean of clinging hair.

For the tail, tie in a small clump of elk or deer hair, but first clean the under fur and short hair from it. The easiest way is to hold the hair by the tips and lightly run finger and thumb of the other hand from tip to butt a few times. Remove any excessively long hair until there are about 15 to 20 hairs remaining. With luck the tips will be fairly even. The tail should be 5/16 inch (8 millimetres) long beyond the bend of the hook, with little or no flare. Cut off the waste butt ends close to the tying thread.

Make a chenille-like strand of dubbing from the green fur, using the technique described in Chapter 6. The strand should be thick enough to form a body about 3/16 inch (5 millimetres) thick. When the dubbing strand is completed, remove the dubbing hook, attach a pair of hackle pliers to the end of the strand, and make two complete wraps of dubbing in front of the tail. Tie off with two turns of tying thread and place the remaining dubbing strand in the material clip. (If you don't have a material clip, just let it hang, but the clip keeps it out of the way.)

Prepare another bundle of hair the same length as the one you used for the tail, and tie it just in front of the last turn of dubbing, making sure that it doesn't flare. Move the thread forward a bit and cut off any excess hair butts. Take a turn of dubbing over the hair, not too tight, and then a firm turn in front of that. Now tie the dubbing down and again place the remainder of the strand in the material clip.

Repeat the operation with the hair again, but hold it a little short of the length of the previous clump of hair—about 3/16 inch (5 millimetres)—and repeat the two wraps of dubbing. Now apply a third tuft of hair slightly shorter than the former, cut off the butts, and take one complete turn of dubbing over the butts. Tie down the dubbing securely, then cut off the unused dubbing.

Tie the hackle feather in by the butt, close to the flue and immediately behind the eye, by tucking the butt under the shank in front of the thread. Holding the feather on edge, take three firm turns of thread over it and cut off the waste butt. With hackle pliers wrap the hackle around the shank three or four times, partly over the last turn of dubbing, crossing the last turn back and forth through the hackle to the front again. Then tie the tip down behind the eye, move the thread through the hackle to the rear, then back again to behind the eye. Form a nice head, then whipfinish. Apply a drop of head cement to complete the fly.

When the hair is correctly applied there will not appear to be any separation between the hair of the tail and the three tufts along the back. Problems most likely to occur arise from a tendency to make the dubbing too generous, along with a too generous use of hair.

When tying down the hair, do so firmly, then trim the butts off close. Hold the hair in a laid down position, then bring the dubbing (not too tightly) over it to the rear of the thread. Now follow with a tighter turn of dubbing over the thread to hold the hair securely. Wrap the thread over the dubbing in two turns to keep it tightly in place, then apply the next bunch of hair in the same way.

Although the traveller sedge is a simple fly to tie, like many patterns it requires patience and practice before a feel for the proper quantities and correct spacing is achieved. Don't despair. Careful work will be rewarded by fishing success.

Water Boatman

Order—Corixa (See page 133.)

The water boatman is common in most small lakes and ponds. It is an air-breathing insect about 5/16 inch (8 millimetres) long and 1/8 inch (3 millimetres) wide. Its head is as wide as its body and is rounded on the front with two large eyes, one on either side, which fit the contour of the head. It doesn't appear to have a neck and its body is flatter than it is wide. It has three pairs of specialized legs— a short pair in front, presumably used in feeding; a longer pair for grasping and holding; and a third, heavily fringed with hair on the outer segment, that are used as efficient oars, hence its name.

The water boatman's colour is a speckled rich brown to a rather greyish brown on the back, with the underside in the adult a medium yellow with a light brown ribbing. The juvenile insect is a pale apple green on the underside, and its body is slightly smaller in size.

Being an air-breathing insect, it carries an air supply in the form of a bubble that encases its underside. When the air supply runs out, the insect makes a hurried trip to the surface. In a fraction of a second the air supply is renewed and it quickly heads for the bottom, the air bubble flashing like a small silver ball.

The water boatman is found in the stomach contents of Kamloops trout for a short period in early spring and for a longer period in autumn. In the spring they do not fly very often, but during calm, sunny days in September they can be seen swimming shallowly in the water and often flying. They hit the water like a drop of rain and immediately disappear below the surface.

A source of confusion to fly fishers is the quite similar back swimmer, which acts like the much smaller water boatman in many ways, even to appearing during identical fall weather of frosty nights and sunny days. There is a major difference between the two, however. In spring the water boatman is an important insect in a Kamloops trout's diet. It is often found in abundance in the stomach contents, while the back swimmer is conspicuously absent.

By contrast, in autumn it is often difficult to decide which insect fish are feeding on. Both are taken in many different ways by the trout. Sometimes, for instance, the fish will take them only near the bottom; at other times they will be taken a few feet below the surface, or frequently just under or on the surface. The fish can be, and most often are, very selective. Even for a person knowledgeable about the insect-trout relationship, it is difficult and time-consuming to solve the feeding pattern.

Adding to the puzzle is the fact that after a day or two of heavy feeding on these insects, the trout will fast for three or four days. And when they start eating again, they are selective. The reason is probably that the water boatman's hard exoskeleton takes a long time to digest—likely three or four days.

When it comes to an artificial water boatman, I feel that many of the patterns are too impressionistic. The following is one of the more successful dressings.

Hook: #12 or #14 Mustad 94840 (Since fish are selective at times, I suggest tying some of each.)

Thread: I like Danville's Fly Master waxed Mono Cord. It is available in 50-yard (45-metre) spools in a number of shades of brown. For this pattern I like a medium brown.

Body: Centre tail feather from a cock pheasant. The best colour is slightly reddish grey. The darker one is usually too red, while the light one is too grey. Try to get one midway between the two.

— Strip of clear plastic, about 1/8 inch (3 millimetres) wide, cut from a Glad freezer bag. Sandwich bags are usually too light and easily torn by the fish, ruining the fly, while the plastic used for storm windows is too heavy and difficult to handle. Lay the bag on a smooth cutting board with a straight edge, and use a sharp knife to cut the strips you need. I use the multi-purpose, snap-off blade cutter available in most building supply stores or hardware outlets.

— Single strand of four-ply tapestry wool in light to medium yellow

Swimmerets: Peacock herl taken from a sword feather rather than an eyed tail. It will have a tougher quill and shorter, less dense flue.

Special Tools: A needle threader, available in most dry goods stores; a pair of small needle-nose pliers; and a beading needle with a large eye, found at most hobby or craft stores. (A beading needle is a long, thin needle used for beading leather, etc. It is round and very thin. Be careful, however, that you are not sold a glover's needle, which is triangular near the point and not suitable for fly tying.)

Begin tying with the hook in the vise at a 15-degree angle. Lacquer the shank with head cement and immediately start the thread. Run it, in spaced turns, down the shank to where the straight portion starts to dip into the bend. Take two turns, trim off the loose end, and let the bobbin hang.

From the pheasant centre tail feather take a section of flue, cut off the tip and butt so as to make a uniformly thick section, fold the section in half, and tie it at the end of the hook shank where the thread hangs, butts to the rear. Three or four turns should secure this feather. Then tie in the plastic strip. With both hands, stretch it just behind the tip until it breaks, thus evenly narrowing it. The plastic can now be tied in securely over this narrow tip without bulking up too much, leaving the main portion strung to the rear and held in the material clip. Run the thread to about 1/16 inch (2 millimetres) behind the eye and let the bobbin hang.

Now tie in a single strand of four-ply tapestry wool, but be careful to maintain the 1/16-inch (2-millimetre) space behind the eye. Grasp the wool with the hackle pliers about 3/4 inch (20 millimetres) from the hook shank and wind the wool to the bend. Take a new hold with the hackle pliers and move the wool forward, overlapping a bit near the middle of the shank, gradually easing the overlap as you approach the eye. Done properly, the result should be a somewhat stout, oval-shaped body with short tapers at either end. Tie it off with three wraps of thread and let the bobbin hang.

If not wrapped correctly, the plastic is inclined to slip much of the time and is most frustrating. The solution is to hold it with hackle pliers or your fingers. Then with enough tension to make it stretch a bit, take a long angular turn or two to the front of the body, a bit more than a half turn around the end (angling to the rear), two turns around the body, then back to the front again. Always maintain the long angled turns until all the wool is covered. It should be done in two passes. The angled turns at either end of the body will keep the wool from slipping off the shoulder of the taper; they will also keep the plastic from slipping. The last pass should end about 1/16 inch (2 millimetres) behind the eye. Now cut off the waste and let the bobbin hang.

Hold the pheasant feather with your right hand and pull it forward over the eye. Put some tension on it, but not enough to make it divide and come down the sides. It must stay on top of the body. With your left hand pick up the bobbin and make two wraps over the feather right behind the eye. Pull it tight, then lift the butt end up and bring the thread in front. Take three or four turns of thread to lock the feather in place, then return the thread to the rear of the butt ends and cut off the waste. Put some head cement on the thread and cut end, build a nice head, whipfinish, then apply head cement.

At about the middle of the body, push the beading needle through, either above or below the hook shank, but don't hit the hook shank with the needle. It is best to push the needle through with needle-nose pliers. When it is most of the way through, put the needle threader in the eye of the needle, then cut 1 to 2 inches (2.5 to 5 centimetres) from the tip of the strand of peacock herl and discard it. Put the remaining piece into the needle threader.

With the pliers, pull the needle all the way through the body. Release the needle from the herl and squeeze the body top and bottom to set around the herl. When it's set, gently sweep the herl to the rear on both sides and cut them off even with the end of the body. They will spring back to a right-angle position, forming the swimmerets.

When the water boatman swims, its legs are held tight to its body and are not visible. There is therefore no need to represent them on this pattern.

The ribbing is optional. I do not always use it, but when I do I put it over the plastic to help make the plastic a bit more durable. Make the ribbing by leaving the waste end long when starting the thread on the hook. Rather than cutting it off, tuck the thread into the material clip until the plastic is wrapped up. Then use this thread to make six or seven wraps of ribbing—and you are ready to challenge that trophy trout.

Mayfly Nymph

Order—Ephemerida (See page 134.)

The mayfly family is a large one, inhabiting streams and still waters in most areas of the world. For the stream fisherman it is probably the most important insect but, sadly, also the most sensitive to water pollution. Before outboard motors became common, British Columbia Interior lakes held vast populations of these insects. Even as late as the early 1960s some waters had superb hatches. Then came the general use of outboards rather than the more aesthetic and environmentally compatible oars. Since then the population decline of this most attractive and important insect has been dramatic. Tragically, today it is rare to see even a fair hatch of this once abundant insect, but there is still some action with well-tied imitations of the nymphal form. In the summer there can be some good sport on the terrestrial imitations of the dun and spinner.

The mayfly most commonly seen on lakes in the Kamloops area is of the *Callibaetis* genus. A small delicate creature, it is typically, at adulthood, about 5/8 inch (15 millimetres) long from the front of its well-formed head to the tips of the two long, upward-curving tails. The first terrestrial stage, called the "dun," appears to pop to the surface in a bubble of air. Then it sits with wings held close together in an upright position, looking like a tiny brown sailboat. The second terrestrial stage is known as the "spinner," and it has a much different appearance. In this stage it is not so often seen on the water, spending nearly all of its short life in the air, flying with a great deal of up-and-down movement commonly called a mayfly dance. Towards evening it can be seen on the water, gossamer wings outstretched from its black body, white tails widely forked as they lie flat on the water. Its brief life span is over.

As can be expected, the dun and spinner stages are represented by dry flies. The nymph stage, however, is a wet-fly pattern.

The *Callibaetis* nymph common to the Kamloops area has a typical body length of 5/16 to 3/8 inches (8 to 10 millimetres), with three long tail fibres. Its gills are located along the back on either side, looking like small paddles aligned in pairs. They alternate between long periods of rapid vibration and short ones of rest. Colour is a pale, greyish, sage green mottled with brown. At times the nymph darts about the bottom vegetation in short, quick bursts of energy; at other times it creeps and clambers about the weeds on long thin legs.

As emergence time approaches, the wing case becomes dark and the insect grows restless. With alternating rapid movement and rest periods it heads to the surface where it leaves the nymphal case, emerging as a dun. Under some weather conditions it emerges some distance below the surface, often popping up in a small air bubble. Although wings on the newly emerged dun appear to be brown, they are actually a slightly brownish-tinted gossamer with dark speckled markings along the leading edge. The nymph feeds on microscopic animals and some vegetation. In turn, along with chironomid larvae, it is a large part of the diet of larger aquatic invertebrates such as dragonfly and damselfly nymphs, shrimp, and many more insect predators.

Hook: A fine wire such as the #14 Mustad 9671 2X long
Thread: Waxed, olive green 6/0
Tail: Cock pheasant tail feather
Body: A pale greyish brown cock pheasant centre tail feather (rather than the more common reddish brown)
Wing case: Cock pheasant outside tail feather (This feather will have the ragged edge of the centre tail feather on one edge; on the inner edge the flue is softer, and it's darker on the underside than the top side.)

Hackle: Hungarian partridge (The small, 1/4-inch (7 to 13 millimetre) body feather, light beige, fan shaped, with medium brown speckling. If possible, avoid the feather with the dark brown bar across it.)

Begin tying with the hook in the vise at the proper angle and lacquer it with head cement. Immediately start the thread a short distance behind the eye and run to the end of the shank where it starts to dip into the bend.

Although the insect's tail is made up of three fibres, we will use four or five. The fish don't seem to know the difference, and should one or even two fibres get broken, the fly will not be ruined. They should be as long as the hook shank. With a few turns of thread secure the tail in position, then take a few turns under the tail to block it up at a 20- to 25-degree angle. Bring the thread back to the original position and let the bobbin hang.

For body material select 10 or 12 fibres of flue from the side of the cock pheasant's centre tail feather and trim off the tips. Then tie them in by the tips where the tail is wrapped down, and carry the thread up to the eye. Carefully wrap the flue around the hook to within 1/16 inch (2 millimetres) of the eye. The body should have a nice taper from eye to tail. If it does not, build up the forward half or two-thirds with a sub-body before wrapping up the pheasant feather. The sub-body should also be tapered so the finished body will be smooth.

After the body material is tied down, wind the thread to the tail and halfway back, using widely spaced turns—five to the bend and three back to the middle of the shank. These turns will help keep the body from breaking up in use. When the thread is in the middle of the shank, take two turns and let the bobbin hang while you prepare the wing-case material.

For the wing case use the cock pheasant's outer tail feather. From the soft side of the feather—the side opposite the one with the ragged edge—take about 3/8 inch (10 millimetres) of flue and roll it so the dark side is to the outside. Cut about 3/4 inch (20 millimetres) off the tip end, and with two or three turns of thread tie the butt section on top of the hook, tip pointing forward where the thread is hanging. Then move the thread in spaced turns to within 1/16 inch (2 millimetres) of the eye and let it hang.

For legs, take the hackle from the side of the Hungarian partridge feather. With the tips of the flue even, pull from the quill a section

3/16 inch (5 millimetres) wide and roll it into a small bundle. Hold it by the butts with your right hand and place it in front of the hanging thread, tips just touching the hook point. Change hands, hold the butts in place, and wind the thread over them, up the near side, loosely over the top, and down the back. Hold it in place with your thumb tip and pull the thread tight. Take two or three more turns of thread, then cut the butts off close to the thread and clear of the eye.

With your right hand pull the wing-case material forward; with the left, pick up the bobbin and drop the thread over it tightly three times, then change hands. Take two more turns, then move the thread in front of and under the waste end. Now take a few more turns to lock it at right angles. Return the thread to the rear of the waste end, then cut the waste feather off. Build a nice head, whipfinish it, and apply a drop of head cement to finish the fly.

Mayfly Dun

Order—Ephemerida, Sub-Imago (See page 135.)
After the dun has emerged, it doesn't move around much on the water except for drifting with the wind, although at times it does remain on the water for some time before flying. It eventually leaves the water and flies to lakeside vegetation to moult, then returns to the lake as a spinner (Imago). In this spinner stage the insect copulates while flying, lays its eggs, and dies. Since the mayfly dun is a terrestrial, the imitation will be a dry-fly pattern. The following instructions will help you dress an effective imitation of the *Callibaetis* dun.

Hook: #14 standard length Mustad 94840
Thread: Medium brown, waxed 6/0
Tail: A large hackle feather from a grizzly hackle cape
Ribbing: Yellow thread or fine oval gold tinsel
Body: Flue from the side of a cock pheasant, centre tail feather
Wing: A light speckled brown feather from a Hungarian partridge body (The larger feathers are most suitable.)
Hackle: Two feathers, both small, from a light to medium brown cape and a grizzly cape. Mature rooster capes are best. This hackle is short, stiff, and requires much less of it to float the fly well on the water.
Dry-fly float: Although it can be liquid or paste, I favour the liquid. I drop the flies in it right after they are tied, then let them dry thoroughly before dropping them in the fly box.

Start this fly in the usual manner, with the hook in the vise at the prescribed angle, lacquered, with the thread run down to the end of the shank where the bend starts.

Make the tail from the largest grizzly hackle you can find. Strip any fluff from the butt end of the quill and any very soft flue. Run finger and thumb lightly down the feather from tip to base to spread the flue. Strip from the quill a section of flue about a 1/2 inch (13 millimetres) wide and gather it into a small bundle. Place it on top of the hook at the bend and tie down with two or three wraps of thread. The tail, from where it is tied on, should be a little longer than the hook shank and should not be straight out from the hook but at about a 15-degree downward angle. Run the thread around the base of the tail material, then carry it down the bend a short distance to force the tail down to the desired angle. This tail not only represents the empty nymphal case, but also supports the rear of the hook so that it has the proper attitude on the water.

Tie the ribbing material in a short distance up the shank, tip to the rear. Now double it back so that its length is strung to the rear, and tie it down firmly.

Take five or six fibres of flue from the cock pheasant's centre tail feather, gather it into a bundle, and cut the tip back about 1/8 inch (3 millimetres). With the tips forward, tie it in on top of the tail wrappings. Carry the thread forward to within the usual 1/16 inch (2 millimetres) of the eye and let it hang while you wrap the pheasant flue to form the body. Tie the body down and cut off the waste. Using hackle pliers, in seven or eight evenly spaced turns wrap the ribbing up to the eye in the reverse direction to that of the pheasant flue and tie it off. Take the thread back to a position about 1/32 inch (1 millimetre) forward of the middle of the body, take two wraps around, and let the bobbin hang.

From a selection of Hungarian partridge feathers, pick two that are as close to identical as possible. On both of them, strip the fluff and lower flue off, leaving about 3/8 inch (10 millimetres) of the top intact. Place them together underside to underside. Holding them in the right hand, put them on edge on top of the shank. With the left hand drop the thread twice over the quills at the base of the flue.

Still holding the feathers on edge with your right hand, use the left to pull the quills until the flue is partly under the thread. Then take two more tight turns of thread over the first turns. With your left hand lift the wing into an upright position. With your right, take four or five turns of thread tight against the front of the feather to block it into a vertical position. Cut the waste quill off and take a turn or two around the base of the now upright wing to hold the flue together—don't pull too tight or it will have the opposite effect and cause the wing to flare. About halfway between the wing and the eye, let the bobbin hang. The wing should be about 3/8 inch (10 millimetres) high. It improves the appearance and balance of the fly if the forward half of the top of the wing is cut at about a 30-degree angle, leaving the rear half rounded.

From the grizzly cape take a small hackle feather whose longest flue is about 1/4 inch (6 millimetres) from the quill to the point. (The feather will likely be about 1 5/8 inches (4 centimetres) long.) Pull the fluff and soft flue from the base of the quill, then prepare a similar feather from a medium red cape the same way.

Holding the first hackle feather by the tip and on edge, tuck the quill under the hook shank and in front of the thread at about a 50-degree angle. Tie it firmly in this position and cut off the waste end. With hackle pliers grasp the hackle by the tip and, keeping it on edge, wrap it twice around the hook close to the back of the wing, and once close in front. Now tie it off and cut off any waste tip.

With one exception, the second hackle feather is handled in the same way. As it is wound through the previous feather, it is wound once behind the wing and twice in front. Carefully holding the hackle out of the way, wrap up a nice head and tie it off. With your fingers, tease the hackle evenly around the hook and trim the tips on the bottom so the fly sits without rolling over to one side. A drop of head cement completes your mayfly dun.

Mayfly Spinner

Order—Ephemerida, Imago (See page 136.)
Although tying the spinner stage of the mayfly is similar in many ways to the dun, there are major differences in material and construction.

Hook: #14 Mustad 94840
Thread: Black, waxed 6/0
Tail: Grizzly hackle quill
Ribbing. White cotton thread, white hackle centre quill, white hair, or fine silver wire or tinsel

Body: Black floss, Phentex, or tapestry wool
Wing: Large, pearl-grey flank feathers of a mallard drake
Hackle: Large and very small grizzly hackle feathers off a good-quality cock cape

Begin tying by placing the hook in the vise in the usual manner, lacquer, and run the thread to the bend. Prepare the tail fibres by taking two large grizzly hackle feathers and pulling the flue off both. Hold them together and tie them side by side, curving upward, about 7/16 inch (12 millimetres) long and spread some 20 to 25 degrees. (Where they should be tied will depend on the size of the feathers and how fine the quill.) After they are tied on securely, take a few turns of thread underneath to cock them in the correct position, and spread them apart by wrapping thread between them in a figure-eight manner. Now cut off the waste quill.

Tie in the ribbing material you have chosen—on this pattern I always use white cotton thread—then put it in the material clip out of the way. Tie on the body material and wrap to the usual place behind the eye. Follow it in the opposite direction with seven or eight evenly spaced turns of the ribbing material. Tie it off, then move the thread into position to tie on the wing, slightly ahead of the middle of the body. Let it hang while you prepare the wing material.

Select a large, pearl-grey, mallard drake flank feather and clean off the fluff and soft flue. Strip about a 3/8-inch (10-millimetre) section from the side of the feather, fold it to about one-third the width, and hold it over the hook with the tips pointing towards the rear. Drop the thread over the feather clump about 9/16 inch (15 millimetres) from the butt end of the feather, and tie it down tightly with three or four turns. Cut the tip off close to the thread, lift the wing up, and with the thread, block it in front tight against the feather. Take two turns around the base of the wing to hold the flue together—not too tight or it will flare. Carry the thread to about halfway between the wing and the eye, and leave it there while you trim the wing to size—about 5/16 to 3/8 inch (8 to 10 millimetres) high, with the front half of the top cut on a 40-degree angle and corners rounded slightly.

The feather is pulled from the quill rather than cut off because it leaves a little of the fibre from the quill on the flue. This fibre helps to hold the butts from flaring while the wing is tied on.

The hackle is prepared in the usual way. Place the butt end of the quill under the hook shank at about a 40-degree angle and in front of the thread. Wrap the thread around the quill at the end of the flue and secure it tightly with three or four wraps, then cut off the waste butt. With the hackle on edge, wrap it twice around the shank. Now with firm pressure immediately behind the wing, bring it to the front, wrap it twice more, then tie it down. Cut the waste tip off, hold the hackle out of the way, build up a nice head, and whipfinish it.

With your fingers, tease the hackle evenly around the hook. Then cut just the tips off the bottom of the hackle to give it a flat base to sit on, preventing it from rolling from side to side. A drop of head cement finishes the mayfly spinner.

Good luck with it.

Damselfly Nymph

Order—Odonata, Sub-order—Zygoptera (See page 137.)

The damselfly is a slow-flying, thin-bodied insect with long gossamer wings. When at rest, its wings are held together, parallel with the body. This position is in contrast to the related dragonfly, which holds its wings at right angles and is much larger. The dainty little damselfly is a very attractive terrestrial. It is usually a brilliant blue with black banding on its long, thin abdomen, although it is often a light brown with black banding.

The nymph lives in lakes and ponds that have abundant sedge grass and cattail along the shores. Here the nymphs climb the plant stems for emergence. Often in June and early July the insects can be seen on shoreline weeds in various stages of emergence, with large numbers of fully developed terrestrials flying about. Kamloops trout have little or no interest in this terrestrial form. The nymphal form, however, arouses lots of interest. When they become active, about a week or ten days before emerging, trout feed enthusiastically on them.

When time for emergence approaches, the damselflies become restless and active, in contrast to earlier stages of development when they remained in one place for hours with little movement. Now they swim to within 12 inches (30 centimetres) of the surface and head shoreward with an energetic sideways movement of their abdomen. After an often long and slow journey they will, with luck,

Rushes and sedge grass, the pantry areas of a lake where in season dragonflies and damselflies are found in abundance.

reach shore where they climb a stalk of sedge grass or other vegetation and emerge into a terrestrial.

The nymph ranges in colour from golden olive to a medium olive green. Its body is up to 3/4 inch (20 millimetres) long and about 1/16 inch (2 millimetres) in diameter, with three paddle-like gills on the abdominal tip. The large head has a large compound eye on either side. The long, narrow wing case sits above a slightly robust thorax from which three pairs of prominent legs protrude sideways when swimming. Strangely, these legs appear to play no part in the forward progress of the insect.

This is a very productive pattern.

Hook: #12 Mustad 79580, 4X long
Thread: Waxed, olive green 6/0
Tail: A large grizzly hackle
Ribbing: White cotton thread, dyed insect green with an ink pen
Body: Golden olive, light Naples yellow, or medium olive green dubbing material
Wing case: A pale grey goose quill dyed a light olive green (You can quickly dye it with an ink pen a small section at a time.)
Hackle: White hackle feathers dyed light to medium Naples yellow or golden olive
Head: The smallest chenille available in a golden olive or light Naples yellow (You can use white and dye it as needed with an ink pen.)

To start this pattern, set the hook in the vise at the prescribed angle and, as usual, coat it with head cement. Then immediately start the thread behind the eye, run to the bend, and let the bobbin hang.

Take material for the tail from the side of a large grizzly hackle feather, after removing the fluff and soft flue. A section 3/4 inch (20 millimetres) wide will make a nice bushy tail. Make it about 3/16 inch (5 millimetres) long and quite bushy by putting your finger on the end and mushing it towards the hook in the direction of the eye. When it is secure, cut off any waste butt. (Wrapping the waste butts down makes it difficult to keep the body as thin as required.)

Now tie the ribbing material next to the wraps that hold the tail down.

Make a very thin length of dubbing in the usual manner (described in Chapter 6) and bring the tying thread to about 1/8 inch (3 millimetres) of the hook eye. The strand will probably still be too thick so, if required, pull most of the dubbing from the dubbing strand after it is completed. Form a body by wrapping the strand in sparse, even turns. Since the head will be large, tie the dubbing off at least 1/8 inch (3 millimetres) behind the hook eye. After tying off the body material, use scissors to trim the body as close as possible to the hook shank without cutting the dubbing thread. Now move the thread back from the rear of the eye 1/4 inch (6 millimetres), take two turns around the hook, and let the bobbin hang.

For the wing-case material, cut a section about 1/4 inch (6 millimetres) wide from a dyed goose quill, double it, and cut the tip back about 3/8 inch (10 millimetres). Tie it on by the tip, the butts to the rear, with three or four firm wraps.

Make a short strand of dubbing as before, and wrap this dubbing on the shank ahead of where the wing-case material is tied to build up the thorax a bit. Tie it down securely, cut off the waste, and trim to a reasonable shape.

Prepare the hackle feather as usual, and holding it on edge by the tip, place it under the hook shank on your side of the thread at about a 40-degree angle. Now bring the thread over the butt, up the side, over the top, down the back side, and pull it tight. Add two more tight turns, then cut the butt off. With hackle pliers, and keeping the feather on edge, take three or four wraps over the length of the thorax, then tie off at the forward end of the body. Trim the top and bottom so there is hackle only on the sides, sticking out at right angles about 1/4 inch (6 millimetres) on either side of the thorax. Should it be a bit too long, simply cut to the desired length.

With your right hand bring the wing-case material forward; with the left hand drop the thread over it twice and pull tight. Change hands and take two more turns of thread, then move the thread around in front. Holding the butts up, lock in place with a few turns of thread in front, close to the wing-case material. Move the thread to the rear again and cut off any waste feather close to the thread. You should now have about 1/16 inch (2 millimetres) of bare hook directly behind the eye on which to tie the head.

From the end of the chenille, strip enough fuzz to bare the two threads. Tie it on by the threads, directly behind the eye, and trim off the excess thread. Now take two wraps of chenille behind the eye to form the head. Tie it off back of the eye and cut off the waste. Bring the thread from the front of the head, over it to the rear, around the shank one complete turn, then over the head again to the front and once around. Repeat this figure-eight wrap three or four times, then whip the head off.

If you have a problem, it will almost certainly be because of spacing or volume. If you follow the foregoing measurements closely, with a little practice you will have respectable imitations emerging from the vise.

Chironomid Pupa

Order—Diptera, Family—Chironomus (See page 138.)

Some authorities claim that worldwide there are more than 1000 members in this insect family. There are four stages in the life of a chironomid fly—egg, larva, pupa, and terrestrial. The egg stage is the least important to the fly fisherman as directly related to the sport. Indirectly, however, it is the stage of greatest importance since without eggs there are no insects. The nearly microscopic eggs are oval with slightly rounded ends and are only visible as small jelly-like rafts on the surface of still water. Shortly after they are deposited on the surface they sink to the bottom where in due time they become larvae—blood worms, described on page 77.

Unfortunately, in the egg stage the chironomid is most vulnerable to the ravages of its worst enemy—man. The oil residue from outboard motors and the indiscriminate killing of many egg-laying adults in the mistaken belief that they are mosquitoes contributes to the wasteful destruction of millions of chironomids and their potential progeny. Many lakes and ponds are sprayed every year for mosquito control when, in fact, the insect destroyed is the innocent, non-biting, chironomid fly. When the loss as fish food is calculated in potential pounds of fish per acre, the magnitude of the damage is obvious. This destruction should be of major concern to everyone, particularly anglers.

For fly fishermen, the pupal stage is probably the most important in the insect's life cycle. They vary in size from about 1/16 inch (2 millimetres) to a little more than 1/2 inch (13 millimetres) long. Black is by far the most dominant colour, but other common colours range from pale watery green to greens so dark they appear black, all shades of brown, and rather pale red to a deep maroon.

The lightly segmented body is thin—a pupa about 1/2 inch (13 millimetres) long will be about 1/16 inch (2 millimetres) thick. It tapers slightly from a short bulky thorax to the tip of its abdomen. On the forward part of its head there is a white plume-like structure that appears on all specimens. I believe it serves as a gill.

Directly under the abdomen on either side there is a short fleshy proleg that wraps close to the body, angling down and to the rear. Although there doesn't appear to be a tail as such, there is at times the appearance of one. The reason is that as the pupa moves to the surface, preparing for emergence into a terrestrial, its abdomen moves forward inside the pupal skin. Then the vacated portion of the pupal case frequently fills with fluid, creating the appearance of a tail. The fluid is frequently coloured but always very pale. This "tail" is short, usually no longer than the body is thick, and, again, is never a dark colour.

Imitating this insect in an artificial involves a number of unique mechanical operations that will be useful in dressing future fly patterns. Materials can vary to a considerable degree owing to this insect's wide range of sizes and colours.

Hook: Mustad 9672, 3X long. Although size is optional, I will use a #14.

Thread: Black, waxed 6/0

Tail: As mentioned, this insect has no tail as such, but there is usually a short bit of the empty pupal case at the tip of its abdomen. To represent this appendage I use a small section of flue from the side of a guinea hen feather. Do not use a feather with white spots. The one with a white webby pattern and tiny white tips on the flue seems to be best.

Ribbing: White cotton thread because it is easily obtainable and the most durable. Never use nylon thread for a white rib. When it is wet it becomes translucent and takes on the body colour. This characteristic practically nullifies the purpose of the ribbing. The centre quill of a white hackle is another possible ribbing. It is durable and has a nice natural taper. But if it is old and dry it may break when you are wrapping it around the body. Fortunately, soaking the quill for 10 to 15 minutes in a solution of 10 percent glycerine and water will usually cure the problem. A long white hair from a moose hackle also makes a nice rib, although it lacks durability. The coarse white hair from a horse's mane or cow's tail is acceptable.

Body: The body can be dressed with wool, floss, fancy-work silk, or cotton. I use black Phentex wool because it is a three-strand product that is easily divided. In addition, each of the three strands can be again divided because the fibres are long and the strands have virtually no twist. This type of material ensures a thin, smooth, nicely tapered body.

Thorax cover: Most often it is sepia to medium brown. I favour natural materials whenever practical, even though they are not the most durable. I have found that their colour is usually slightly muddy and more natural in appearance than any of the artificial dyed materials. For this reason I use dark, turkey-tail feathers; Chinese pheasant tail feathers, male or female; or any other feather that seems appropriate for colour and modelling characteristics.

Thorax: It is short and bulky, slightly larger in diameter than the abdomen, and a bit longer than it is in diameter. On most patterns I have found peacock herl to be satisfactory for both colour and convenience. On very small patterns, however, it may be too bulky. One or two strands of flue from a cock pheasant tail feather are a satisfactory substitute.

Proleg: Because this appendage is quite difficult to tie on properly, many tyers leave it off, reasoning "Oh, it doesn't make any difference whether it is there or not." Admittedly, while the difference over a season is perhaps small, on a tough day a proleg can be the difference between success and complete failure. I think it's worth a little effort—so, obviously, do the fish. Almost any dark body feather from a small bird—hen teal to an immature starling—will make a proleg. I prefer the starling because feather size is about right for most patterns and I like the bronze tips. Some of the better fly-tying supply companies carry these feathers on the skin.

Gills: The gills are two white tufts of delicate, soft fibres that appear to be joined until they are examined closely with a glass. Gills are an important fixture on all chironomid pupae and really should be represented in successful imitations. Most often the feather used to represent gills is herl off a white ostrich or emu plume. I don't like these sources because the material mats after one use. Thereafter it has the appearance of a piece of string wound around the head—most unrealistic. A soft white wool—Angora or any of the many synthetics—is much better. They are not inclined to mat, and many synthetics seem extremely white, in fact almost fluorescent.

Begin the pattern with the hook in the vise and lacquer it with head cement. Immediately start black thread at the eye and run it to where the shank just starts to dip into the bend. Prepare a guinea hen body feather by stripping the fluff and soft flue from the base of the quill. Then take a flue section about 3/16 inch (5 millimetres) wide and strip it from the quill—after you have teased it down to a position at right angles to the quill until the tips are even. Make a small bundle, and holding it by the base in your right hand, place it on top of the hook shank with not more than 1/8 inch (3 millimetres) protruding beyond what will be the end of the body. This is the short tail. Change hands, and keeping the tail material on top of the shank, tie it down. Next, run the thread to within 1/8 inch (3 millimetres) of the eye. If any of the guinea hen feather is not tied down, cut it off close to the thread. Now wrap the thread back to the bend in well-spaced turns.

For ribbing, tie in by the end a 2- to 2 ½-inch (5- to 6-centimetre) length of white cotton thread, using four or five firm wraps. Now run the tying thread up to within 1/8 inch (3 millimetres) of the eye.

If you have black Phentex wool, cut off a 6-inch (15-centimetre) length and separate the strands. Divide one of the strands in half, then tie it on the shank about 1/8 inch (3 millimetres) from the eye. If you are using black tapestry wool, divide it into individual strands and use a single strand. When building the body, hold it short—1 to 1 1/2 inches (3 to 4 centimetres)—with hackle pliers and take the twist out. In this way thickness can be controlled and a smoother body will result. The Phentex wool can best be wrapped with your fingers.

Tie the wool in where the thread hangs, and wrap thinly and firmly to the bend, covering the thread that holds down the tail and rib material. Now reverse the direction of the wool, being careful not to have a lump where the material reverses to go back to the eye. Increase the diameter of the body slightly and gradually as the wool nears the position from where it was started. Move the thread to within 1/16 inch (2 millimetres) of the eye, then bring the wool to it in a smooth taper and tie it down. Cut the remainder off and take a few more wraps of thread to tie down any wild fibres. Let the bobbin hang about 1/16 inch (2 millimetres) from the eye.

Now hold the ribbing thread with hackle pliers and in five to seven—never more—evenly spaced turns wrap the rib up to the tying thread in the reverse direction to the body material. (I've explained the reason for this in the instructions for the blood worm fly.) Take two turns of thread over the rib material, double it back, add two or three more turns, and cut off the remaining thread. The end will now be locked in.

For the thorax cover, cut a 1/8-inch (3-millimetre) wide strip of flue off a dark, turkey tail feather. Cut 3/8 inch (10 millimetres) off the outer end and place the feather on top of the hook, with the cut outer end about 1/16 inch (2 millimetres) from the eye and the remaining feather trailing back over the bend. Tie this feather down firmly on the end, working the thread to the rear about 1/8 inch (3 millimetres), then take two extra turns, working back a bit towards the eye. Now let the bobbin hang.

You will need two small body feathers to represent the prolegs. As mentioned, I use a starling feather with a tiny bronze tip. Strip the flue off both sides of the quill to within 1/4 inch (6 millimetres) of the tip, brush both sides of the remaining tip with head cement, and immediately stroke it to a spear-like point. Put it on a piece of wax paper to dry while preparing another feather. (If you are going to tie several flies, make a large number of these proleg feathers at a time. Then clean the glue from your fingers with acetone or lacquer thinner. This method saves time since you aren't continually cleaning cement off your fingers. Remember to use acetone or lacquer thinner in a well-ventilated area away from fire.)

The proleg feathers are now fairly stiff, and the flue is not likely to separate as they are tied on. Take one feather and place it on the far side of the thorax area, tip pointing down and outer side of the feather to the outside. It should angle rearward to follow an imaginary line from eye to barb. It should also be barely long enough for the tip to be slightly below the body and wrapped slightly under to meet the next feather you tie on in the same way on the near side. Hold the feathers in the desired position and take four or five careful but firm wraps of tying thread. With practice it is not a difficult manoeuvre, but to be effective it must always be done with care.

Select one strand of peacock herl and break off 3/8 to 3/4 inch (10 to 20 millimetres) of the tip. (Breaking the strand off now is better than having it break when almost wrapped on—which it usually does.) Tie it in by the tip and take about three turns of the herl to build a small stout thorax to just cover the thread that holds the proleg on. Tie it off, figure-eight the thread over it twice, and let the bobbin hang.

Now take the tying thread to about 1/32 inch (1 millimetre) behind the eye, then pull the turkey feather forward over the peacock herl and the proleg butts. Pull it tight but not so that it splits and tends to come down the sides. Hold it firmly in this position and take two tight turns over it. Then hold the end of the feather up, move the thread in front of it, and take a number of turns between the eye and the feather. Return the thread to the original position behind the flue and take two more turns to lock it in position. Now cut off the feather and apply a tiny bit of head cement.

Tying in the gills completes the fly. Cut a 2-inch (5-centimetre) length of white tapestry wool, separate the four strands, and carefully divide one. Lay it across the shank immediately behind the eye and in front of the tying thread. Carry the thread over the wool and in front of it, then around the shank to the front of the wool, back over it, and behind it on the far side in a figure-eight wrap. Repeat a few times, then pull both sides of the wool forward. Hold them together and cut them off short so there will be about 1/32 inch (1 millimetre) on either side. Whipfinish the head and apply a drop of head cement, but don't get any on the gills. The fly is now ready for fishing.

Caution: Three firm wraps of tying thread are adequate to securely hold most material. Additional wraps only add to bulk, and on small flies this unnecessary bulk makes finishing off difficult.

Sedgefly Pupa

Order—Trichoptera (see page 139.)
Of the three stages of the sedgefly's life span, the pupal stage may be the most important to fly fishers. This is when it is most vulnerable to fish predation. In the larval stage, for instance, it is well camouflaged, and as a terrestrial it can fly off, preyed upon more by birds than by fish.

The pupa, after it has left the larval case, may remain among the bottom weeds for two or three days before embarking on its slow and perilous journey to the surface. Here it may swim just under the surface for some time before emerging. It holds its wings erect to dry and may take directly to the air. More often, however, it skitters about the surface for some time before flying.

There are many species within the order and great variety in coloration, specific behaviour, and size. Size ranges from 3/16 inch (5 millimetres) to as large as 3/4 inch (20 millimetres). Colours are as varied as the sizes, from creamy tan to greyish brown and all natural greens from bright emerald to a rather dark olive. Colour combinations are also common: a green abdomen, for instance, with cinnamon thorax, head, legs, and embryo wings.

The sedgefly most commonly imitated in the Kamloops area, the fly-fishing capital of Canada, is the large one commonly called the traveller sedge (genus *Phryganea*). The pupa is very large, its average length slightly under 3/4 inch (20 millimetres), with a small head in comparison to the rest of the body. Its legs are held tightly along the underside with the exception of the swimmerets, which are long, at right angles to the body, and shaped somewhat like rowboat oars. Antennae the length of its body sweep to the rear down either side. The embryo wings slope down and rearward past the halfway part of the body, while the abdomen tapers from a rather portly posterior to a much smaller diameter as it joins the thorax.

The pupa's colour is somewhat varied, usually a medium sage green but occasionally olive green. It seems the larger the pupa, the darker the colour. The lines between segments appear to be a medium yellowish tan and quite thick.

Hook: #8 Mustad 9672, 3X long. Hook size is optional. A #10 79580, 4X long, is only slightly shorter than the #8 9672, 3X long, but there is a great difference in the depth of bite and the diameter of wire.

Thread: Danville's Fly Master waxed 6/0 in medium brown

Ribbing: Medium yellow embroidery silk. Silk ribbing material comes in small hanks the same as fancy-work cotton. The silk, however, is quite shiny, four ply, and remains shiny when wet.

Sub-Body: Tapestry wool in the same or close to the same colour as body material (A light shade is preferable to a dark one.)

Body: A medium sage green dubbing material. Ideally it would be seal fur dubbing of a light to medium sage green—sometimes called "mole." But since seal fur is almost unobtainable, one of the modern substitutes will serve well.

Thorax cover (wing case): Hen pheasant centre tail feather. The thorax cover is not intended to represent a wing case. It is simply to cover where the imitation embryo wings are tied in and should match, as close as possible, the colour of the wing packets.

Hackle: Golden pheasant tippet, or Chinese cock pheasant saddle hackle. Although the legs are not very visible, I feel the addition of this hackle contributes towards the impression of life.

Embryo wings: Small beige and brown breast feathers from a wild duck, the hen teal. (Colour should closely match that of the hen pheasant centre tail feather used for the thorax cover.)

Swimmerets: Chinese cock pheasant saddle hackle. (Because of the length and closeness of the antennae to the swimmerets, it is not practical to represent both. We therefore eliminate the antennae.)

Begin tying with the hook in the vise at the prescribed angle. Lacquer the shank, then immediately wrap on the thread behind the eye. In spaced turns take it down the shank to the bend. Cut off the waste end and let the bobbin hang while you prepare the silk ribbing material.

Divide the strands of a 4-inch (10-centimetre) length of silk embroidery thread, tie two in at the bend of the hook, and drop the length into the material clip.

For the sub-body, take a single strand of the four-ply tapestry wool, about 2 inches (5 centimetres) long, and tie it on the shank about 3/16 inch (5 millimetres) from the bend. Run it back to the bend, move it forward two or three turns, tie it down, and cut off the waste. Now in spaced turns move the thread back to the bend over the sub-body, then let the bobbin hang while you get the dubbing ready.

On the dubbing board prepare a row of material of modest proportion. When wrapped on the hook it should build a body about 3/16 inch (5 millimetres) across over the sub-body, gradually thinning to 1/8 inch (3 millimetres) for the forward portion of the body as it approaches the hook eye. Tie the dubbing strand off 1/16 inch (2 millimetres) from the eye and cut off the waste. With scissors trim the body smooth and to the desired shape.

Now you can remove the two strands of silk from the material clip and twist them clockwise into a single strand. Wrap this ribbing for about six or seven evenly spaced turns over the body in the opposite direction to the body material. Tie it off at the end of the body 1/16 inch (2 millimetres) from the eye, and let the bobbin hang.

From the side of the hen pheasant centre tail feather, take a section about 3/8 inch (10 millimetres) wide, fold it in half, and cut the tip back about 3/8 inch (10 millimetres). Bring the thread back a bit and tie in the feather by the cut tip. Take the thread over the feather to about the halfway point of the body and take two or three firm turns. Bring the thread halfway back towards the eye and let the bobbin hang.

Now prepare the embryo wings so they will be ready after the legs (hackle) are in place. Take two small teal breast feathers and pluck them until the length from tip to base of the flue is about 1/2 inch (13 millimetres). As mentioned above, if you plan on tying a number of flies, prepare enough feathers at the same time. A piece of waxed paper, stapled or taped to a 6-inch (15-centimetre) square piece of stiff cardboard, is excellent for holding feathers while they dry.

When the feathers are ready, put a generous drop of head cement on the middle finger of your left hand, take a feather by the prepared stem of the butt, and place the flue on the cement. With finger and thumb work the cement into the flue, mould the flue into a spearhead shape, then place it on the waxed paper to dry. It will not stick to the paper and is easily available when required.

The next step is to take about 10 fibres of either long tippet flue or cock pheasant saddle hackle flue and place them on the underside of the hook so that the tips just reach the point of the hook. Tie them in tightly, close to the eye, easing up on pressure as you move a few turns to the rear. Then move to the front in the reverse manner and trim off the waste butts. Be careful to maintain the head space of 1/16 inch (2 millimetres) behind the eye until the thorax cover is pulled forward.

To tie in the embryo wings take one feather and place it on the far side of the hook. Slope it down and to the rear so that it almost reaches the point of the hook and curves toward the underside. Tie it securely with three turns of thread and cut off the waste stem. Now place the other feather on your side of the hook and repeat the process so they are both even.

You can now pull the thorax cover forward to cover the wrapping that holds the embryo wings in place. Pull it fairly tight so that it does not bulge upward, and tie it down behind the eye with three or four turns of thread. Then tip the butts up and take a few turns in front of them to lock the feather. Return to the original position, then cut the waste butts off.

To imitate the swimmerets, tie in five or six fibres of cock pheasant saddle hackle, about 1/2 inch (13 millimetres) long, on either side at the head. They can stand out at almost right angles to the body. Secure them in place with a few turns of thread, then cut off the waste butts. Add a drop of head cement, build a nice head, and whip it off. Add another drop of cement and you are ready to challenge that trophy trout.

Emerging Chironomid

Order—Diptera, Family—Chironomus (See page 140.)
As a pupa, the chironomid fly rises vertically from the lake bottom to the surface. Here it rests briefly at an angle until the pupa moves forward a bit and the case becomes parallel to the surface. The head now splits open lengthwise, leaving a section of white plume on either side. The newly emerged terrestrial stays just in front of the empty case for a few moments, the tip of its abdomen overlapping the head of the empty case. When its wings dry it flies off to mate, then lay eggs.

While the wings are still soft the chironomid is particularly vulnerable to fish and birds. During prolific hatches, swallows, ducks, and other birds gorge themselves on untold thousands of chironomids. Fish do not seem greatly interested in the emerging insects, apparently preferring the pupae. But during light hatches or late in the day when emergence is nearly over, fish take them quite readily.

After a heavy emergence the distinctive empty cases thickly cover the still water long after the hatch is over. This is an important clue to the fly fisherman, but empty mayfly cases are often confused with those of the chironomid. The major identifying feature is the shape of the mayfly's body. It is much more tapered and has three tail fibres that are half to two-thirds the length of its body and well spread out. By contrast, the chironomid body is less tapered with no tail, and at the head of the empty case there are the distinctive and highly visible white plumes on either side.

The Emerging Chironomid is a very successful pattern when well tied.

Hook: #14 Mustad standard 94840 or the slightly longer shank 9671—both are fine, forged wire hooks with a tapered eye

Thread: Black, waxed 6/0

Tail: Pearl mallard breast feather or male teal breast feather. Pearl mallard is the large grey feather from the side of a mature mallard drake, usually from under the wing. The teal feather is almost the same and from the same place, although the dark markings can be much darker and larger, and have more contrast than the mallard.

Body: Peacock herl taken from the eyed tail or a bundle of strung herl. The strands of herl from an eyed tail often have a brassy colour. In addition, the flue on each strand is a lot longer than herl from a sword feather, desirable for this pattern. By contrast, the flue from the sword quill is usually a brilliant, almost fluorescent emerald green, not suitable for this pattern.

— White wool, either four-ply tapestry wool or one of the synthetics

— A cock pheasant centre tail feather that should be greyish brown, not one that leans heavily toward reddish purple

Ribbing: Very fine gold or silver wire tinsel (optional)

Hackle: Any red cock hackle that is natural, dark reddish brown with the flue short enough for such a small hook, preferably from a cape

Begin tying as usual with the hook in the vise at a 15-degree angle. Lacquer it with head cement and immediately start the thread right behind the eye. In spaced turns run it to the end of the shank above the rear of the barb.

From a mallard breast feather take a 1/4-inch (6 millimetre) section of flue and form it into a roll about 1/16 inch (2 millimetres) or a bit less in diameter, and about 3/4 inch (20 millimetres) long. Although the chironomid has no tail as such, this flue represents the empty nymphal case, which appears tail-like when the pupae emerges. Tie it on the hook so it will extend 7/16 inch (11 millimetres) beyond the bend of the hook, and hold it down with three or four turns of thread. Let the bobbin hang and trim off any remaining butt.

Take three or four strands of peacock herl that have good solid tips and tie them in at the tail, the tips extending about halfway into the mallard tail. Tie them down so they do not flare but lie close and tight to the mallard feather. The main length of the strand should extend towards the eye.

Now fold in half a section of flue about 1/4 inch (6 millimetres) wide from the pheasant tail feather. Cut off about 3/16 inch (5 millimetres) of the tip. Then tie the cut ends in over the peacock herl at the bend, the butt of the feather to the rear.

Twist together, counter-clockwise, several turns of the tying thread and the peacock herl, then wrap the thread/herl strand around the hook to form a thin body. Separate the herl from the thread, tie off the herl, cut off the waste, and return the thread to the bend of the hook. Here, if you desire, the fine tinsel wire can be tied in at the bend and locked so it will not pull out.

Tie in a single strand of the four-ply white tapestry wool by laying it across the hook shank at the bend above the barb—directly on top of all the previous material. Figure-eight the thread over it so that it stays at right angles to the shank. Cut it off on either side of the hook so it will be about 1/16 inch (2 millimetres) long on either side. Bring the thread forward to about 1/16 inch (2 millimetres) from the eye and let the bobbin hang. In spaced turns bring the tinsel up the body and tie it off.

Prepare a 1 1/4-inch-long (3 centimetre) hackle feather from a dark red rooster cape by removing the fluff and soft flue. Then hold the feather by the tip and lightly draw your fingers down the feather from tip to butt to spread the flue at right angles to the centre quill. With the feather on edge, place the tip under the shank and in front of the thread. With three firm turns, tie it in solidly and cut the waste tip off. Grasp the butt with hackle pliers and wrap it around three times. (The smaller diameter of the quill's tip is tied in rather than the thick butt to reduce bulking at the head.) Tie the feather off and cut off the waste.

You may take a few more turns, moving the thread back and forth through the hackle to end up immediately behind the eye. With finger and thumb work the hackle into a beard. Cut off any flue that is on top and will not stay down. With your left hand sweep the hackle down and back, then lay two turns of thread over the butts to hold the hackle in place.

Pull the pheasant tail forward over the top of the body and, keeping firm pressure, drop the tying thread around it and pull tight. Take two turns, then holding the butt up, bring the thread in front and take a few more turns to block the feather in that position. Bring the thread behind the feather again and cut off the waste close to the thread. With a few turns of thread, cover the cut end of the feather and form a head as small as possible. Whipfinish, add a drop of head cement, and go fishing.

Shrimp

Order—Amphipoda, Family—Gammarus (See page 141.)
Commercial shrimp patterns are seldom well designed or well tied. The body is often strongly curved, the hackle representing the legs far too long and extremely bushy, colours are ridiculous, and the fly too large. A fish would have to be either retarded or blind to accept such a pattern.

In reality, a shrimp's body is not strongly curved when in motion. It has only a slight suggested curve, most pronounced at the rear third. The only time its body is strongly curved is when it is at rest, holding on to a weed or some other object. It has a lesser curve while feeding. It captures its food while swimming, grasping it with its front appendages. Then it stops swimming, and as it tumbles through the water while devouring the food, its body will curve.

Although the largest specimen I ever saw was about 9/16 inch (15 millimetres) long, adult Gammarus shrimp most often are 3/8 to 1/2 inch (10 to 13 millimetres) long. In cross-section its body is oval, almost twice as deep as broad. It has a hard exoskeleton with overlapping plate-like segments, a large number of legs, and four moderately long antennae projecting from the front of an ill-defined head. Colour is a pale, rather translucent, muddy olive with legs tending towards a muddy yellow. I have seen red and also pink shrimp, the colour depending on diet. When it feeds on chironomid larvae (blood worms) or tiny, red, water mites, the nearly translucent body takes on the colour of material in the digestive tract.

Yellow shrimp are nearly always mature specimens near the end of their life. On a few rare occasions I have seen robin's egg blue shrimp, but I don't know why they were this colour. In addition, I have many times seen them opalescent pink and blue, the result of light reflecting off the exoskeleton much as it does off mother-of-pearl. When you study trout stomach contents, realize that colour becomes more pronounced as digestion progresses. Yellow shrimp can end up appearing orange.

Hook: Hook style is optional. While I prefer a #10 Mustad 94840, Sproat 38930 is also a good choice, although the longer curve of the bend gives the body more curve than I like.

Thread: A pre-waxed, olive green 6/0 doesn't bulk up too much and is very strong. Olive green is better than standard black, which detracts from the natural appearance, especially if the head is large.

Ribbing: Almost any clear, fine monofilament that you might use as tippet material. I use 4-pound (1.8-kilogram) Stren simply because I have a good supply and find it satisfactory.

Body: Hen pheasant centre tail feather is my best choice for colour and durability. Although white-tail deer hair is a good colour, it is unfortunately not too durable.

— A 3/16-inch-wide (5 millimetre-wide) plastic strip some 4 3/8 inches (11 centimetres) long from a large, clear plastic, freezer bag. First cut a 5-inch (13 centimetre) square section, then make strips 3/16 inch (5 millimetres) wide.

— Should you be fortunate enough to have a supply of seal fur in the proper colour, use it for your dubbing (as already mentioned, commercially it is called mole). You will find it does not absorb water or change colour, but reflects a natural light. There are some reasonable substitutes on the market in a wide selection of colours. Use a muddy, pale to medium olive green.

— Any tapestry wool close to the same colour as the dubbing material. Exact colour is not important, although it should be reasonably close. When tied on top of the hook it should be about 1 1/2 times the diameter of the wire to give the fly the proper dimensions by building up the back. One strand of four-ply tapestry wool is suitable.

Begin the fly with the hook in the vise at a 15-degree angle, barb just clear of the jaws. Lacquer the shank with head cement and immediately start the thread just behind the eye. In spaced turns run the thread to the bend and let the bobbin hang directly above the rear of the barb.

Tie a knot in a 12-inch (30 centimetre) length of monofilament close to one end, then tie it on the hook where the thread hangs. Use two turns on either side of the knot so that it cannot be accidentally pulled out. The monofilament will be used to rib the fly, but for now place it in the material clip out of the way.

Move the thread one-third of the way towards the eye and tie in a 4-inch-long (10 centimetre-long) single strand of tapestry wool by the end, length extending over the eye. Twist the strand until it is tight—it should be about the same diameter, or slightly larger, than the wire of the hook shank. Now bring the thread tightly—in spaced turns—to within 1/8 inch (3 millimetres) of the eye and tie down the wool. Bring the wool, still twisted tight, back over the original pass. Return the thread in evenly spaced turns to just past the original starting point and tie the wool down. What you want here is a bit of tapered padding on the top of the fly body. To get an even taper, it helps to let some of the twist out of the wool strand just prior to reaching the original starting point. When properly done there should be an even, short taper with no bump. Cut off excess wool and take a few extra turns of thread to tie down any loose fibres.

Now remove the fluff and soft flue from the base of a quill of pheasant tail feather. Tease the flue down to a right-angle position to bring the tips of the flue even. Close to the quill, take off a section of flue about 3/8 inch (10 millimetres) wide and fold it to about one-third that width. Lay it on top of the hook tips, pointing over the bend about 1/4 inch (6 millimetres). Now tie it down firmly where the shank starts to dip into the bend with three or four tight turns of thread. Then work the thread towards the eye for a few turns and let the bobbin hang.

Cut a plastic strip, pointed like a fence picket. Lay it on top of the pheasant tail, point towards the eye, and tie it in by the point. Catch the length of it in the material clip along with the monofilament to keep it out of the way.

Now double the pheasant flue so that it lies to the rear of the bend. Just behind where it is doubled, tie it down tightly. Be careful. Tying too close to where it is doubled causes the thread to slip off when the feather is drawn forward to make the back. Bring the thread forward until it is just off the pheasant tail.

Make a dubbing strand from the seal fur in the usual way. Caution: Your strand of dubbing likely will be overly generous. Since it is simple to add material but difficult to subtract, it is better to be miserly.

Carefully wrap the dubbing around the hook, starting as close as possible to the pheasant tail, each turn close to but not on top of the previous one, to the end of the wool. Take one turn in front of the wool and tie the dubbing down. Cut the remainder off and take two turns of thread to tie down any loose fibres. Then trim the back (not too close) into a slight curve, with both sides flat. Use the dubbing needle to pick and comb the underside, then trim to the depth of the gape of the hook.

Next pull the pheasant tail forward over the top to form the back. Holding it so there is no slack, tie it down securely behind the eye. Do not cut the waste feather off any closer than 3/16 inch (5 millimetres) from the eye. If you do, the feather will pull out from under the thread at the eye as you wrap the ribbing up the back, ruining the fly. Done correctly, there will be no thread showing at the bend.

Now bring the plastic over the back and draw it tight so that it stretches over the back. It will then pull down each side a short distance. Be sure to keep it even. Tie it off behind the eye with three or four firm turns and cut off waste as you did the pheasant feather.

With the monofilament, take one complete turn around the hook clockwise above the end of the tail. Then carry on over the plastic in evenly spaced turns to simulate body segments. As the monofilament is brought underneath, move it back and forth sideways to prevent wrapping down the dubbing material that will form the legs. Holding the thread and bobbin out of the way, whipfinish the monofilament and put on a drop of head cement. Cut off the pheasant feather and plastic immediately behind the eye, but be sure the eye is not obstructed. Build a nice head with a few turns of thread over the monofilament, whipfinish, and add another drop of head cement. With the dubbing needle, clear any cement out of the eye.

If the underside is too thick, carefully thin it with sharp, finely pointed scissors until there is a reasonably close resemblance to legs.

Finally, with your thumbnail on top of the tail fibres and your index finger underneath, draw the thumbnail over the fibres with modest pressure to curl the tail fibres upward. With the scissors parallel along the back, cut the tail off at the desired length, leaving it with a slight curl. Finally, with the dubbing needle pick out any fibres that may have been wound down that represent legs. The fly is ready for casting.

Dragonfly Nymph

Order—Odonata, Sub-Order—Anisoptera (See page 142.)

The dragonfly is one of the largest insects flying around the lakes. It has four gossamer wings level with, but at right angles to, its body and high on a large bulky thorax. Its abdomen is long and thin, about 2 3/4 inches (7 centimetres) overall. Body colour is a brilliant aqua with a pattern of black markings. Rarely seen to rest, it catches and eats smaller insects while flying.

In the hundreds of fish stomachs I've examined over the years I have never found the terrestrial form of this insect. The nymphal form, however, forms a major part of a trout's food and this form is what we will imitate. As fly fishers, we are interested only in the readily visible features of this insect—form, colour, movement, and habitat—we will leave the microscopic details to professional biologists.

The dragonfly nymph is the largest insect regularly found in fish stomachs. Although a large nymph can be up to 1 3/4 inches (4.5 centimetres) long, most specimens are about half that size. Its head is up to 5/16 inch (8 millimetres) wide, including large compound eyes on either side. The thorax is narrower than the head, slightly deeper, with embryo wings protruding tent-like over the back for a short distance. Wing length depends on the stage of development. At its longest, just prior to emergence, the wing is about 5/8 inch (16 millimetres). On the lower side of the thorax are three pairs of long, strong legs.

The dragonfly's abdomen is rounded on top and basically flat on the bottom, up to just over 1 inch (26 millimetres) long from the base of the rear pair of legs to the tip of the spike-like guards that protect the rectal orifice. At the widest point, near the fourth segment from the tip of the abdomen, it is up to 3/8 inch (10 millimetres) wide. When swimming, its long legs are held close to the body and reach as far back as the fourth of the nine body segments.

As for many aquatic insects, the environment dictates body colour to a considerable degree. In clear-water lakes with grey, stony bottoms, dragonflies are often a medium greyish sage green. On lakes with bottoms of chara and/or nitella weed, a rather dark, greenish olive predominates. Brown water lakes with small dead trees and brush along the shore and sparse green bottom growth produce nymphs coloured tan, brown, and sepia.

On their backs, most nymphs have what I can describe only as "lines of angular dark markings parallel to the central axis of the body." For a time, when they have shed their hard exoskeleton and before the new outer covering hardens, they are a medium to pale watery green—their large, black, compound eyes contrasting strangely with a pale body. Always shy and secretive, they are far more so when they shed. They seem to realize how vulnerable they are until the outer covering hardens and they regain their protective camouflage.

In the nymphal stage they creep slowly over the lake bottom while hunting the wide range of insects on which they feed. At other times they lie in ambush under a rock or in the cracks and crevices of underwater logs and boulders. Often they will move rapidly from place to place using a unique form of propulsion—their respiratory system. The nymphs take water into their abdomen, where oxygen is extracted and the water is then expelled through the rectal orifice. This water serves as a powerful jet that moves them quickly in a stop-and-go fashion for relatively long distances. I have watched large nymphs move in bursts of from 5 to 7 inches (10 to 18 centimetres) for several feet before resting.

Dragonfly nymphs adapt to a wide range of environments, although some lakes seem to be more favoured than others. The ideal environment is a lake with good weed cover for insect life and an abundance of bulrushes and sedge grass up which the nymphs can clamber when emerging.

When it emerges, the nymph climbs out of the water, up a weed stem, shoreline tree, or fence post. Here it waits for its skin to dry and split lengthwise from its head and along the back of the thorax. It first frees its head, then thorax and legs. Then it adjusts the legs and takes a firm hold on the nymphal case head. It rests often, then, with an arching of thorax and slowly emerging abdomen, draws its tightly folded wings and long abdomen completely free. In 20 to 30 minutes the insect will be fully developed and will fly away to prey on many small flying insects before mating and laying eggs.

The greatest predators of dragonflies in their nymphal state are humans and fish. Some birds also feed on the nymphs and newly emerging terrestrials. The large numbers of these insects in small bodies of water not inhabited by fish give an idea of the extent they are used as fish food.

Hook: #6 Mustad 79580 or #6 Limerick 3665A. The latter is a long shank hook slightly longer than the 79580. It is the longest hook I use for any pattern. When a smaller fly is required I use the #8 or #10 gape but stay with the 79580 4X shank.

Thread: Olive green, dark brown, or black depending on body material colour, in 6/0 waxed

Ribbing: Fine copper wire or fine oval gold tinsel

Sub-Body: Any tapestry wool close to the colour of the finished body

Body: Dubbing material in peacock olive or brown olive, both medium tone. If you can find seal fur it is best; otherwise, a commercial product is an acceptable substitute.

Thorax Cover: A light-toned brown, white-tipped turkey tail feather or a dark, hen pheasant tail feather
Thorax: Bronze peacock herl as opposed to green herl (It will have to be picked out of a bundle of strung herl since I've not found it available as a separate colour.)
Hackle: Hen pheasant centre tail feather
Head: Peacock herl

Start the fly by clamping the hook in the vise at a 15-degree angle, barb clear of the jaws. Brush the hook with clear lacquer head cement and immediately start the thread just back of the eye. Run it in spaced turns to where the shank starts to bend (directly above the barb), and let the bobbin hang while you prepare the tail material.

Although the nymph has no tail as such, we must represent the short, sharp spines that guard the orifice. To do so take a small pinch of dubbing between finger and thumb. With the finger and thumb of your opposite hand pull it apart and place it back together again. Repeating this process two or three times will make most of the fibres lie parallel. With your left hand place this material on top of the hook in position for a tail and take two firm turns of thread around it. Pull the material in your left hand just hard enough to leave some fibres tied down by the thread. Repeat as many times as necessary to form a bushy tail, which we will later trim to shape.

Ribbing material can be tied in now or after building the sub-body. Take a 4- to 5-inch (10- to 13-centimetre) piece of fine oval gold tinsel or fine copper wire and tie it in by the end, length extending over the eye. Using two turns of thread tie it down, then double the main strand back so that it strings over the bend. Take two or three more turns to lock it in place. Now move the tying thread to the middle of the hook shank and let it hang.

The purpose of the sub-body is to give the body shape and conserve expensive dubbing. Beware of making the sub-body too robust. As already noted, it is better if it is somewhat skinny. To start the sub-body, cut about 5 inches (13 centimetres) of tapestry wool of the desired colour and separate the four strands. With hackle pliers take one strand and tie the end in at about the middle of the shank, not more than 1 1/2 inches (4 centimetres) between hook shank and hackle pliers.

Wrap the wool tightly around the shank and taper it to both ends. The thickest point should be 5/8 inch (16 millimetres) to the rear of the eye. The long, thin taper should end on the forward end

3/16 inch (5 millimetres) from the back of the eye, and the rear taper should end about 1/8 inch (3 millimetres) from where the shank starts into the bend. The middle of the sub-body should be as close as possible to 1/8 inch (3 millimetres) thick, with an even, longish, curving taper to either end. Arrange to tie off at the end of the rear taper. Now take a few well-spaced turns of thread back and forth over the sub-body, finishing at the end of the rear taper. These turns will hold all the wraps in place. Let the bobbin hang while you prepare the dubbing and thread to build the body.

While I prepare the dubbing strand on my pant leg, other tyers have a 6-inch (15-centimetre) square piece of plywood covered with denim pants material stapled on, which works well. Place a pinch of dubbing on the board and tease it into a narrow row about 3 inches (8 centimetres) long and 3/16 inch (5 millimetres) wide. Now pull the bobbin until there is about 6 inches (15 centimetres) of thread between bobbin and hook, and rub the dubbing wax full length. With the bobbin in your left hand and the thread taut, carefully pick up the dubbing and put it on the half of the thread closest to the hook. Rest the end on the hook shank so that it will not be inclined to roll to the underside of the thread, and gently press it so that it sticks to the thread.

Make a dubbing strand in the usual way, ending up with a strand about half as thick as medium-sized chenille. Twist it quite tightly. Now you can use either the dubbing hook or hackle pliers to hold the dubbing while you wind it around the hook. Start wrapping the dubbing over the thread that holds the tail in place, then continue to wrap, being careful to keep the turns tight against the preceding ones without climbing on top. At the end of the sub-body take one more turn, then tie it down and cut off any remaining dubbing material.

Take a few more turns to secure any loose fibres, apply a drop of head cement, and let the bobbin hang. There should be about 1/8 inch (3 millimetres) of bare hook between the end of the body and the back of the eye. Now is the time to shape the body. With sharp, well-pointed scissors and being very careful not to cut the ribbing or the tying thread, trim the underside close and flat. Keep in mind that the widest part of the body should be 5/8 inch (16 millimetres) from the back of the eye. It is best to have it closest to the hook bend rather than the eye. Now trim the back in a long slope from the eye to the widest body part, then down the rear slope to include the tail. Follow this shape on either side. If the trimming is done correctly, the body should be squarish. Now round it off, being sure to bring the tail to an even, natural point.

Use hackle pliers to wrap on the ribbing in a direction opposite to the dubbing. If it appears to become hidden in the dubbing, do not be concerned. All that is required to be effective is a glint here and there. Make five to seven evenly spaced wraps of the ribbing, tie it off, and lock by doubling it back and taking two more turns. Then cut the remainder off and let the bobbin hang.

For the thorax cover cut a 5/8-inch-wide (16-millimetre-wide) section of flue from the turkey tail feather after stripping the fluff and soft flue from the base of the quill. Before cutting it off the quill, tease it down to a right-angle position to bring the ends even. Fold it to about 1/4 inch (6 millimetres) wide, then cut about 3/8 inch (10 millimetres) off the end. Take the tying thread back over the dubbing to 1/4 inch (6 millimetres) from the rear of the eye, then lay the tail feather on top of the body, cut the end even with the end of the dubbing and the long end towards the bend. With four or five tight turns of thread secure it in this position. Then run three or four spaced turns forward almost to the end of the feather and let the bobbin hang.

Now select four or five strands of bronze peacock herl, cut about 3/8 inch (10 millimetres) off the tips, and tie in at the end of the turkey tail. Twist the peacock herl and the tying thread together four or five turns and wrap it back to where the turkey feather is tied down. Then return to the original position. Next separate the thread from the herl, figure-eight the thread over the herl twice, and cut off the remaining waste. Take two more turns to anchor the loose ends of herl and let the bobbin hang.

The next step is the hackle feather to represent legs. As always with a new feather, strip the fluff and soft flue from the base of the hen pheasant centre tail feather quill, even the ends, then take 12 to 14 fibres of flue from the quill. Hold this flue by the butts in your right hand and place it under the peacock herl thorax, tips reaching to the hook point. Change hands and tie it down, firmly for the first two or three turns, then progressively looser for a few turns as the thread moves to the rear. Return the thread to the starting point in the reverse manner. At this stage the hackle will likely not be exactly where it should be, but don't be alarmed. If it is not too far out of position it can be worked into the correct alignment.

Now pull the turkey feather, which will represent the embryo wing case, forward over the herl thorax. Keep this feather tight with your right hand, and carefully drop the bobbin twice over the turkey tail feather, then pull it tight. Change hands and take two more turns. Hold the waste end up, move the thread to the front of the feather, and take several turns to block the feather at right angles, locking it in place. Return the thread to its original position, cut off the waste, and put a drop of head cement on the wraps.

The head is the last operation. If all the spacing has been followed closely it should be easy. Select three or four strands of peacock herl and break off an inch or so (26 millimetres) of the tip, tie them in by the broken-off ends behind the eye, and form a ball about 3/16 inch (5 millimetres) around. Figure-eight the thread over the herl and cut off the waste. From top to bottom the head should be rather flat, with a suggestion of separation between head and thorax. Carefully take two or three turns of thread behind the head to create the impression of this separation. Then, again with careful thread placement, figure-eight for several turns to create the illusion of large compound eyes. Whipfinish the head, add a drop of head cement, and select a lake to try your handiwork.

It is highly unlikely that the first attempt will be to your liking. The major faults are usually spacing and volume. It is somewhat frustrating because an error in volume will compound the spacing problem and vice versa. But take your time and don't get discouraged. Remember, professionalism is the reward of practice.

Gomphus Dragonfly Nymph

Order—Odonata, Sub-Order—Anisoptera (See page 143.)
Dragonfly nymphs of the genus *Gomphus* (red-shouldered dragonfly) are seldom found in the stomach contents of trout, but not because they are unpalatable. Trout seem to relish them. The reason is that this nymph is very shy and effectively hides in the marl or weeds on the lake bottom. In most Interior stillwaters the nymph is therefore not readily available to fish. Just before its emergence to adult form, however, it abandons its reclusive ways and moves towards shore, becoming highly vulnerable to trout predation.

At shore, the nymph climbs on any available bush, tree, rock, or even a cabin wall. When it has found a suitable place to cling, it waits until its outer skin dries and splits over the head and down the wing case. The insect lifts its head out first, then the legs. Now it takes a firm hold on the head of the case and slowly draws out its rapidly lengthening abdomen, the wings immediately starting to unfold. In about 20 minutes it flies off, a fully developed terrestrial.

Since the nymph is the only stage of the *Gomphus* dragonfly's development fed on by trout, it is the subject of our imitation.

The nymph's lightly segmented body is spider-like in appearance, with a short broad abdomen, large head, long legs, and a wing case that is not really noticeable. Its abdomen is flat on the underside, strongly curved on top, and appears to have short hair on a body often covered with small bits of bottom debris, giving it an unkempt appearance.

Colour is, to some extent, dependent on the immediate environment. Most often it is a medium grey with a slight medium olive green cast on the upper body, and a darker stripe on each side of a centre line. The flat underbody is a dirty, pale to medium yellow, tinged with pale insect green. The embryo wing case is the same colour as the body and up to half as long.

Its head is somewhat triangular. The neck and the mouth parts (labium) have a narrow appearance, accented by a dark bar across the top of its head, looking something like a mask. Its eyes are small and hardly noticeable.

Hook: #8 Mustad 9672, 3X long

Thread: Medium grey, olive green, or tan

Body: A combination of deer hair and seal fur, or a seal fur substitute, in a medium light olive

Hackle: Flue from the side of a hen pheasant centre tail feather (When separated, it has a modelling very like the natural markings on the insect's legs and is soft enough to move authentically when the fly is drawn through the water.)

Other materials: Two dye-fast ink pens—one a light to medium avocado; the other a light yellow

This fly is a slow, tedious one to tie. A hurried approach means you are simply wasting your time.

Start with the hook in the vise at the regular 15-degree angle, but do not lacquer it because the body material has to be able to slide on the hook shank as it is applied. Put a tiny dab of cement on the shank above the barb and start the thread there. Take three or four wraps, cut off the waste thread, and let the bobbin hang.

From a patch of deer hair cut a small bunch about 1/8 inch (3 millimetres) in diameter. Holding it by the tips, stroke out the loose hair and under fur. (Here you will require the plastic bag or anti-static material, described in the traveller sedgefly instructions, clamped near the vise to clear loose hair clinging to your hands.) Lay this clump of hair across the hook shank to the rear of the thread so there is about 3/16 inch (5 millimetres) of the ends on the far side and at right angles to the shank. Tightly figure-eight the thread around it to keep it at right angles and cut off the remaining hair the same length on your side of the hook. With the remaining hair repeat the procedure twice more. Let the bobbin hang.

Prepare a dubbing that will be as long as the deer hair on the hook, even, and fairly sparse. With a back-and-forth movement through the deer hair, wrap it to the rear two turns, then forward in the same way. Next drop two turns of thread over it to keep it from unwinding. Clamp hackle pliers to the end of the dubbing so it will not untwist, and hold it out of the way. With your finger and thumb at the bend to prevent the material from going around it, push the hair tightly together with a twisting motion. Continue applying deer hair and dubbing as before until it is about 3/16 inch (5 millimetres) from the eye. Now wrap it down securely, tie it off, and cut the bobbin loose. Lacquer the knot, turn the hook over, and prepare to shape the body.

Now comes the possible frustration. If the clumps of deer hair were small enough, all is well. But if they were large, you will have a problem. The thread will not be close to the hook shank and will likely be cut when you trim the body to shape, ruining the fly.

Be brave. Trim the underside as tight as possible and flat. Now turn the hook over and shape the top side. The body, in profile from the top, should be a slightly elongated egg shape, the widest part situated between one-quarter and one-third the distance from the rear tip of the abdomen. The back is slightly rounded from side to side, tapering quite quickly from the greatest width to the rear, with a longer, more shallow taper forward.

Caution: There is usually a tendency to make the body much too robust.

Put a bit of head cement on the thread where it was cut off and restart it, then let the bobbin hang while you prepare the hackle.

From the side of the hen pheasant tail feather, pull or cut five or six strands of flue. Place them in position on the far side of the hook, angling downward and just reaching the point of the hook, then tie off securely. Repeat the procedure on your side of the hook and run the thread to a position behind the eye.

The head is built with deer hair in the same manner as the body. Trim it flat on top and in the front—about 3/16 inch (5 millimetres) wide, tapering back to the neck area. The face also has this triangular shape, widest at the top and narrowing to the mouth area. It has an overall size of approximately 3/16 inch (5 millimetres) on the hook we have used.

Now you need two dye-fast ink pens—one a light to medium avocado; the other a light yellow. With the former make a narrow line on either side of the centre, lengthwise along the back on the head, and draw a light line from side to side across the top front, the widest part. Then with the light yellow pen, colour the belly portion. Finally, rub the fly all over with a small piece of soft cloth to blend the colours a bit and soften the edges. And that's it.

Good fishing.

Nation's Red Dragon

(See page 144.)

I am not a fan of flies that do not imitate trout foods, but I used them when I first began fly fishing and know that some of them still produce trophy trout on occasion. It's been a half century since I last used such flies, but I think this book would be incomplete without mentioning at least one old-time favourite.

The Nation's Red Dragon is an original pattern given to me by my friend Jack Carmichael, who often fished with the legendary Bill Nation. This pattern was one of Bill's more popular flies during the early 1930s and well into the 1940s. Used extensively at Paul, Knouff, and Badger Lakes during this period, it was a favourite of a lot of old-timers and during its popularity produced many fine catches of trophy trout.

Bill Nation favoured rather large hooks and a variety of bend styles. Hook sizes 4, 6, and 8 were popular with Bill, who used them with sproat or limerick bends. Most often, because of the style of the hook bend, he tied a rather short body. On many of his flies he used a silver tag, which served to accent the appearance of the short body.

It may be an interesting experience to fish with some of the old favourites once again. Tying them is also good fun and involves techniques useful for tying imitative patterns.

Hook: #6 Mustad 3906, sproat, turned down, tapered eye, hollow point, bronzed

Thread: The original was black 4/0 silk; today I would use one of the modern synthetic threads in a 6/0 black

Tail: A section taken from a teal flank feather

Body: Rear half silver tinsel; forward half red seal fur dubbing, or substitute

Wing: A section of the brown flank feather from a male hooded merganser duck

Wing topping: Narrow sections of flue taken from a pair of red-dyed goose quills

Hackle: A medium-sized, soft, badger-coloured hackle

With the hook in the vise, lacquer the shank with head cement and start the thread behind the eye. Run it in spaced turns to where the shank starts to dip into the bend, take two extra turns, and let the bobbin hang while you prepare the tail material. With the tail material a bit longer than the size of the hook gape, tie it securely where the bobbin hangs. Cut off the waste butt and tie in a piece of flat tinsel about 3/32 inch (2 millimetres) wide and about 5 inches (13 centimetres) long. Run the thread to within 1/8 inch (3 millimetres) of the eye and let the bobbin hang. Wrap the tinsel so it will cover the thread that holds the tail, then continue up the shank, completely covering it to where the bobbin hangs. Tie it down with a few turns of thread, cut off the waste, and let the bobbin hang.

Prepare a bit of the red seal fur (or substitute) for a sparse dubbing. Then bring the thread back to a point half way on the tinsel, take two extra turns, wax the thread, and make the dubbing in the usual way. Run it in slightly spaced turns over the tinsel to the forward end and tie it off. Let the bobbin hang and prepare the merganser flank feather for the wing.

From the side of this feather take a section of flue approximately half an inch (13 millimetres) wide and fold it in half. Hold it in position on top of the hook and take two turns of thread over it. Put a drop of head cement on the wraps of thread, then add three more firm turns. The cement makes it unnecessary to cinch the thread so tight that it causes the wing to flare, and when dry will hold it securely in place. Trim the waste butt off and let the bobbin hang while you prepare the red goose quill sections for the topping.

Two sections of the goose quill are required, one from the right-hand feather and one from the left, with each section about 1/8 inch (3 millimetres) wide. They are placed one on either side at the top of the wing and of the same length—the end of the wing should be long enough to reach the end of the tail. With the outer side of the feathers to the outside, tie them in place in the same manner as the wing.

Select a medium-sized, soft, badger-coloured hackle and strip from the base the fluff and very soft flue. Place the quill under the hook shank and close to the flue, on edge with the outside of the feather facing forward. Tie it securely in this position, then cut off the waste end. Keep the feather on edge, take three turns behind the eye, and tie it off. Now hold the flue back and build a nice head tight against the hackle. Tie it off, add a drop of head cement, and file it away for use on a day when your best imitators fail. Or perhaps for a time when you just want to fish as the old-timers did.

Have a happy time!

Making the Flies 129

Woolly Worm (Sedgefly Larva)
(see page 75)

130   Tying Flies for Trophy Trout

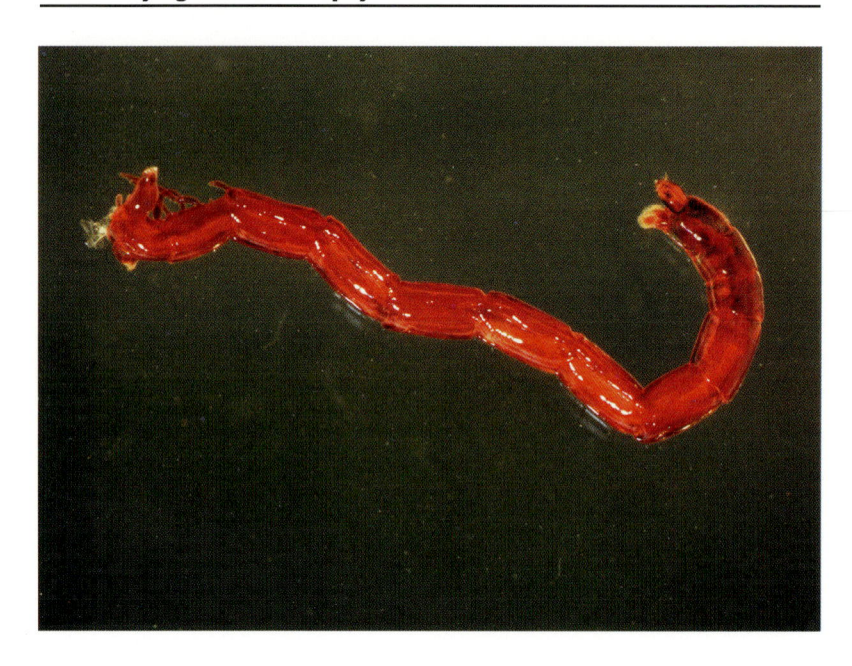

Blood Worm
(see page 77)

Making the Flies 131

Leech
(see page 81)

Terrestrial Traveller Sedgefly
(see page 84)

Making the Flies   133

Water Boatman (see page 87)

A source of confusion to fly fishermen is that the quite similar back swimmer, lower right, acts in many ways the same as the water boatman, top right.

134   Tying Flies for Trophy Trout

Mayfly Nymph
(see page 91)

Making the Flies 135

Mayfly Dun
(see page 94)

Mayfly Spinner
(see page 96)

Making the Flies   137

Damselfly Nymph
(see page 98)

Chironomid Pupa
(see page 102)

Making the Flies 139

Sedgefly Pupa
(see page 107)

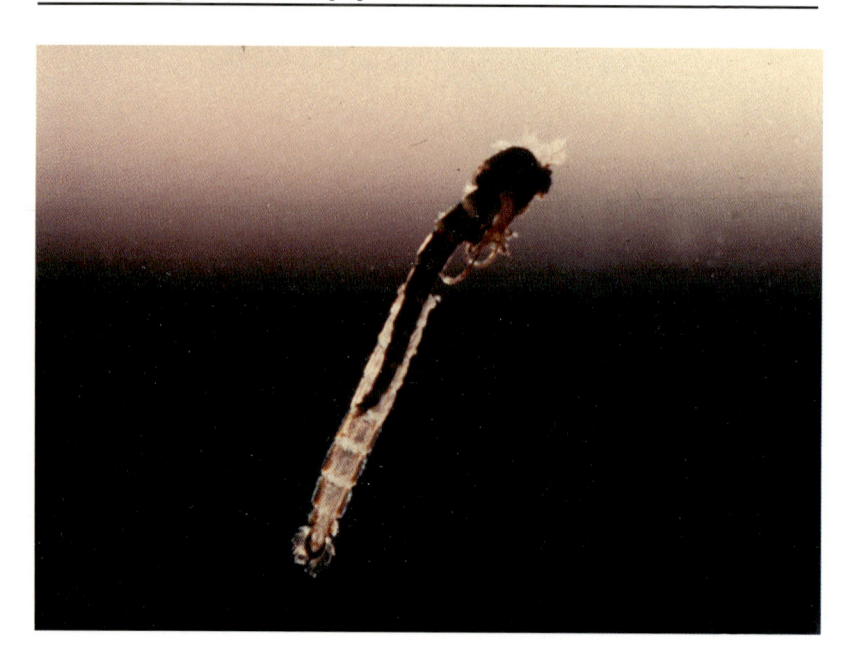

Emerging Chironomid
(see page 111)

Making the Flies 141

Shrimp
(see page 114)

142   Tying Flies for Trophy Trout

Dragonfly Nymph
(see page 117)

Making the Flies 143

Gompus Dragonfly Nymph
(see page 123)

Nation's Red Dragon
(see page 126)

Two Tone Chironomid
(see page 144)

PART FOUR

A CLOSER LOOK AT CHIRONOMID FISHING

Fishing chironomid imitations is not always the best way to fish, but it often is. On many days it is also the only way to catch trout.

Chapter 11

In The Beginning

Observant fly fishermen have always known about chironomids. They are extraordinarily abundant on virtually all trout lakes, and trout feed heavily on them most of the season. Oddly, though, no Kamloops-area angler seems to have seriously attempted their imitation until the early 1960s at Heffley Lake. So far as I can tell, chironomids were similarly ignored in most other areas as well.

Back then, Heffley Lake had just recovered from the poison used to eliminate coarse fish. The toxaphene had done that job well, but it seemed to have also impacted the lake's invertebrate population. Most of the standard trout foods were temporarily in short supply—so short that a group of us transplanted several species of invertebrates to the lake. Gammarus shrimp seemed especially hard hit and took a long time re-establishing themselves. That's likely why the lake soon had such a huge population of chironomids. Shrimp and other invertebrates avidly feed upon chironomids, so with reduced predation their populations exploded. The newly re-introduced trout naturally fed avidly on such bounty. Lack of other food forms must also have increased trout attention to chironomids.

Since we then knew nothing of chironomid fishing, great frustration occurred.

Heber Smith, however, was selling (and using) a fly called the Brown Quill. It's really just a Carey Special with a black body ribbed with white, but in small sizes it produced quite well at times. Then Jamie, Heber's son, discovered that by chewing most of the hackle off, it worked even better. That seemed odd, but when I started examining the stomach contents of trout I caught, I discovered that none of the ingested food items had wings.

The author's fly-tying bench.

So I started tying the flies without any hackle, with no improvement in success. I re-examined my specimens with a hand lens and discovered that while the colour and shape were about the same as a de-hackled Brown Quill, they had a tiny proleg on either side of what looked like a very large head. Hmmm. So I tied a head of peacock herl, and underneath it angled two pieces of flue from a mallard duck quill. I trimmed them short to imitate the prolegs. I tried them, though I doubted they'd make much difference.

The result was astonishing. The new fly was a tremendous success, but I still wasn't satisfied. I'd noticed that the specimens all sported a tiny white plume on the front of the head, so I decided to add this to my pattern. Again, it improved the fly. I've made various alterations since then, ending up with the pupal imitation described on page 102.

Imitations of other chironomid stages followed that first fly, and techniques for fishing them developed over time. The major breakthrough occurred, though, on a day we were fishing a large shoal. The water was clear and about five to eight feet deep, with trout visibly cruising over the marl, singly and in pairs. Every so often a school of six to ten fish would cruise by. Mostly they simply swam past, but occasionally a trout would dart to the side, take something, and then continue on its way.

Our first casts to those trout were totally ineffective. Back then we presumed trout would ignore a motionless sunken fly, so we naturally retrieved our flies. We tried many different retrieves but all seemed to have the same result: trout moved away. The trick was to not move the fly. We eventually found that by casting 15 to 20 feet ahead of a cruising fish and letting the fly sink (resisting the urge to at least twitch the fly), the fish would take it into its open mouth.

Setting the hook remained a problem. A set was definitely required, but we missed many fish before realizing we had to wait until the trout's mouth closed on the fly and the fish started to turn. Then all that was required in the way of a strike was a lifting of the rod to take the slack out and the battle was on. As we progressed, we found we had only to watch the line where it entered the water. When it moved, we lifted the slack out of the line and the fish was on.

Many other refinements have occurred over the years (and continue to be developed) but the basics were well established by the mid-1960s. As such, I'm regularly amused by magazine articles describing this NEW fishing method.

Chapter 12

Chironomid Gear

Chironomids in all their stages can be fished with standard tackle and equipment, but real proficiency demands some special equipment. This equipment is useful for any fly fishing, but it is especially so when offering chironomid imitations.

You need two anchors. With just one anchor your boat will sway in the wind and you lose control of your fly. That's always a problem, but with chironomids it is fatal. If the boat moves enough to pull the line sideways to any degree, trout will certainly ignore your chironomid imitation. Keep in mind that chironomids rise straight up to the surface and do not move sideways. Any horizontal movement is therefore unrealistic and trout simply ignore what I presume they do not recognize as a true chironomid. Trout are perfectly consistent about this. Oddly, though, trout will take a fly falling straight down about as well as one rising straight up. Strange.

Should you choose to fish chironomids in water more than ten feet deep, a wrist watch that displays seconds is another necessity. You have to know where your line is, and that requires timing the line's descent. Few people are accurate in estimating time. In fact, my experience suggests that a person told to wait two minutes before starting to retrieve line will start retrieving in less than 30 seconds—unless he or she has a watch.

You'll also need lines capable of sinking to the required depth, and you'll need to know just how fast they sink. If, for example, you want to fish near bottom in 30 feet of water, a fast-sinking line will take, depending on the manufacturer, about three minutes to reach bottom. In this case, you should start a very slow retrieve at about 2 minutes and 45 seconds. The fly will continue to drop for a few seconds after you begin retrieving. It will be pulled quite unnaturally along the bottom for awhile after that, but it will

This small boat is all set-up for chironomid fishing

eventually begin rising straight upward. This is the time to expect a strike, but please realize the strike will not be dramatic. The fly just stops and you'll note only a twitch of the line, a slight movement of the rod tip, or a bit of unnatural weight on the line. Strike quickly or the trout will be gone. Without careful attention you might not even know you've had a strike.

A piece of rubber or a commercial leader straightener is another absolute requirement. If a leader is not perfectly straight, the fly can be moved three to six inches without signalling anything to the fisher. Since trout reject fraudulent chironomids very quickly, an angler using a kinked leader can therefore draw a hundred strikes without ever knowing about them.

The standard small boats used for any lake fly fishing are quite appropriate for chironomid fishing, but it's especially important to add some carpeting and move as little as possible. Pupal and emerging chironomid imitations are often fished near the boat, so you really must minimize alarming vibrations. Keep in mind, too, that deeply fishing imitations are worked almost directly below the boat. Your boat had best seem completely harmless.

Chapter 13

Altered Chironomid Flies

The chironomid patterns described in Chapter 10 are all reliable and much-used patterns, but you often need to alter them a bit. The following three stories should illustrate that point, as well as provide three flies that, under the right conditions, can prove invaluable. They might also suggest why this fishing is so fascinating.

Black Chironomid with Gold Rib

My friend the late Heber Smith bought the fish camp on Salmon Lake and moved there from Heffley Lake in 1969. I would drive out most weekends and fish with Heber. He was usually busy at things I could not assist with, so I spent much of my time fishing alone. I usually fared quite well.

There were a tremendous number of chironomid in the lake, and my standard pupal imitation produced well enough to keep me happy. However, not being willing to leave well enough alone, I one afternoon noticed a lot of chironomid emerging around the wharf at the resort. I got my specimen jug and aquarium net, found a dry spot to lie down, and spent an hour watching the pupae rise to the surface. I then netted several of them and put them into the specimen jug—covering it to block out light and delay the pupae's emergence as long as possible.

Back at the cabin I continued to study those insects. They looked like the chironomids I was familiar with at Heffley Lake, but I eventually noted a dramatic difference. These pupae had bodies with five or six segments of equal width, and some of them had alternating bands of glistening gold and shiny black.

I tied up a fly to imitate them—a simple matter of replacing the white rib on my standard pupa with flat gold tinsel about 3/64 inch (1 millimetre) wide (see bottom of back cover). It looked good so I tied up a half dozen more and gave some to Phyllis (Rusty) Smith, Heber's daughter, just as she was on her way out for a couple of hours' fishing. I went back to the cabin and watched the last of my captured pupae emerge into terrestrial form. Insects really do fascinate me.

Later, on the dock, I got into a conversation with a gentleman who had just come in. He said that, while fishing was pretty good, there was a young lady out on the lake who was really killing the fish. I was curious but I learned a long while ago that too intense an interest causes some folks to clam up and others to embroider the truth. So rather than asking what the young woman was using, I asked who she was. The angler said he didn't know her but she certainly knew how to handle a boat and a fly rod.

Having my suspicions, I watched for Rusty's return. Seeing me waiting, she exuberantly jumped out of the boat almost as soon as it hit the dock and excitedly showed me her fine catch of trout. She reported strikes on almost every cast but, knowing Rusty, I put off much of her report as exaggeration. I wasn't nearly as impressed as I should have been. The next day, when I fished the new pattern, Rusty's words came back to me. Just as she reported, fish struck on virtually every cast.

Two Tone Chironomid

It was early June and my friends Ralph and Elaine Shaw, Ted Smith, and Horace Miller were visiting for the weekend. They naturally planned to fish. I'd done well at Tunkwa Lake a week or so earlier, but Tunkwa is often crowded on weekends. Leighten Lake, I thought, would draw fewer anglers, so that's where we met.

Perhaps Tunkwa was more crowded that weekend, but maybe not. Leighten Lake held enough fishermen to make me wonder how we'd fare with so many boats and so much competition.

I had something of a secret weapon, though—a new fly I'd tied after my last trip to Tunkwa Lake. On that trip I'd found that the stomachs of the trout I'd kept were stuffed with fairly large chironomid pupae (about #12). On casual inspection they seemed the standard black colour, but after separating them in a glass of water and holding the best specimens up to good light, I could see the abdomens were a dark to medium green with the thorax a much paler green. Where the two colours met there was a blending of tones, the darker green gradually becoming lighter until it was a very pale watery green at the head. On some of the specimens another change was evident. Where the body had begun to move forward in the case, the vacant pupal skin at the tip of the abdomen had some red fluid, which I found contained haemoglobin.

Tying an imitation involved just a few changes from my standard pupa. The carapace, prolegs, and gill structure needed no alteration, but I substituted a red body feather from a golden pheasant for the standard guinea fowl fibres. I coloured the white cotton ribbing a pale green by rubbing a Pantone #375F waterproof ink pen over it before wrapping it on the body. For the body and thorax I used a medium forest green and a pale apple green wool (see middle of back cover or page 144).

On the lake, I gave my friends some of these flies. In very short time we were all playing fish. Later, on shore, another friend who was camped at the lake came down to tell us how amusing it was to watch the antics of the other boats trying to position themselves to catch fish. This friend, Bob McShane, said at one point he counted 14 boats, all fishless, going around us.

Half Pink Chironomid

In the mid-1970s I spent time fishing Roche Lake. On the camp side of the island, at the far end of the lake, there was a shoal where some good fish could be seen cruising. They seemed to be feeding—taking sub-surface insects with a darting movement and occasionally coming to the surface with a lazy rolling movement.

I presumed the trout were taking chironomid pupae. There were a number of large chironomids hatching, and the swallows were taking those insects daintily off the surface without raising a ripple. I captured a couple of the adult chironomids and, since they were a dark greyish to black colour, presumed my standard black-bodied pupal imitation would be a good choice. I fished it a good long time but it was essentially ignored. Thinking perhaps a different line would better present it, I switched from a slow-sinking line to a sink-tip, and later tried a floater. I generally prefer a slow-sink line, but the other lines can sometimes allow more effective presentations. One trout finally struck my imitation—fished dead on a floating line (bobber fishing) but that was the only action.

When I cleaned the trout and examined its stomach contents, the cause for my lack of success became obvious. The trout had indeed been feeding on chironomid pupae of the size I expected, but the pupae were a reddish pink colour, which closely matched my flush of embarrassment. I should have at least suspected something like this. While the adults I examined were blackish grey in colour, I had noticed that the newly emerged adults seemed a reddish brown colour, almost maroon. In just a few seconds the wings became grey, though, and the reddish colour disappeared.

So, of course, those reddish wings would pretty much have to create a reddish thorax area in the pupae.

I naturally tied some flies to imitate the reddish pupae, simply copying my standard pupa but substituting a thorax of medium to deep pink fancy-work cotton (Mouline 3326) for the thorax portion of the body (see top of back cover). One of these was the first fly I tried on the next day.

There were, however, no fish to be seen on the shoal nor any of the red-winged chironomids. It was a full hour before the first red wing appeared. I was watching it quite closely, ignoring my line, when the reel clicked a few times. I looked down to see that the line, which had been coiled at my feet, had disappeared and a trout of about 2 1/2 pounds was now taking line from the reel. Trout don't often hook themselves on chironomid imitations, but this one did and he was magnificent. After landing the trout, I continued to fish with the new fly and had excellent fishing—so good I soon tired of harassing the fish and went home to tie some more flies.

I thought I now had a very useful fly, but as so often happens, I didn't see those reddish chironomids again for a number of years and caught nothing when I tried the fly. One evening, though, I told the story to my friend Horace Miller and gave him a few samples of the fly.

Good thing I did.

About two years later, Horace and I were fishing Jacko Lake and having a really tough time of it. Around two in the afternoon we noticed the swallows were picking up the odd small fly from the surface. I fished hard, trying everything reasonable and a few things unreasonable, before eventually hearing Horace whoop. I looked up to see a really fine, silver fish in the air, attached to Horace's line. The fish kept Horace busy for some time but, fish finally in the boat, Horace looked up and said one word: "Pink."

Tunkwa Lake

The light chop hitting the side of my boat made hearing difficult, so I pulled up anchors and rowed over to Horace. As I came alongside him, he again said, "Pink." He then told me he had seen a reddish brown chironomid taken by a swallow and recalled my Roche Lake story. A bit of searching disclosed the fly I had given him and, yes, it worked.

I rowed back to where I'd been, dropped the anchors, tied on a Half Pink Chironomid, and started to catch fish. We had a week of superb sport on the Half Pink before Horace had to return to Vancouver.

Chapter 14

Thoughts in Closing

We as fishermen—and, I hope, as sportsmen—must always treat with respect and dignity the trout we catch, whether they are released or dispatched for table use. If they are to be released they should not be played to exhaustion, but handled as little as possible, preferably without being removed from the water. Barbless hooks (easily made by crushing the barb of the hook down with a pair of needle-nose pliers) help too. And some restraint seems essential. Releasing hundreds of trout has to produce significant mortality and seems to me disrespectful. Completely eliminating the hook point can, however, allow release with virtually no mortality. You still get the strike and perhaps a run and jump or two. The fly comes loose then, but no matter. You've had the best of the fishing experience without causing any harm.

Should you choose to keep a fish, it must be dispatched quickly, immediately put on ice, and cleaned as soon as possible. It will then make excellent table fare. Left in the sun in the bottom of a boat it decomposes rapidly and soon is not fit to eat. The worst possible treatment is to drag still-living trout alongside the boat in a sack or on a stringer. The trauma of rough handling and confinement results in a very poor quality fish. More importantly, no living thing should be treated with such cruelty and indignity. I emphasize that if a fish is to be kept, it deserves to be killed as quickly and painlessly as possible. To have a fine trout flopping around in the bottom of a boat or on a stringer reflects the callous attitude of the person responsible for its suffering.

Be courteous to your fellow anglers. Treat others as you would like to be treated; especially avoid crowding and other interfering. Many fishermen do not like to be asked what they are using, and if asked will rarely tell the truth. When you don't ask questions, many

Contrary to what many anglers believe, large lakes can offer excellent fly fishing. B.C.'s third largest natural lake, for instance, is Kootenay, some 85 miles (136 kilometres) long. In 1977 it yielded B.C.'s largest fly-caught rainbow— 25 pounds, 2 ounces (over 11 kilograms).

anglers will volunteer information and you will get truthful answers. Be friendly, use your own knowledge and expertise, and often someone will help you if you're having a tough time.

It is vital for us to care for the environment. There are many ways to help—not littering, keeping fuel out of the lakes, cleaning up messes left by others, and joining a club devoted to protecting trout waters and quality angling experiences. Contributing to environmental care not only will add to the pleasure of fishing but, more importantly, will also ensure that your grandchildren will inherit something of value, not polluted streams and barren lakes.

Consider abandoning the internal combustion motor on small lakes where it is quite unnecessary. I think such motors are among the most damaging of all things used on small lakes. In terms of pounds of fish per acre, the loss of emerging insects and their potential progeny because of oil film is staggering. When you consider as well these motors' extremely offensive odour, noise, and surface disturbance, they truly do seem a curse inflicted on trout lakes. For the person who feels incapable of rowing a small boat, an electric motor is an efficient, odourless, light-weight, and convenient substitute.

Carrying out garbage is much more important than many anglers realize. I've found ducks and fish hopelessly tangled in discarded fishing line, cut and painfully strangled to death through the thoughtless action of some fisherman. The simple matter of tossing a bottle cap overboard can produce a dramatically littered bottom and cause trout mortalities, both directly and indirectly. Nothing should be left behind.

A bag of some kind can be used in the boat to store waste conveniently so it can be carried home and disposed of in the trash can. Because there is no garbage collection at our lakes, do your share to protect them from trash. As already emphasized, our world belongs to our children. They will inherit only what we leave them. Will it be a mess or a clean, productive system of lakes?

Should I, with this book, have helped to improve your enjoyment of fly fishing and helped to protect it, my effort will have been rewarded.

Fishing Regulations

Freshwater Fishing in British Columbia

British Columbia has Fish and Wildlife offices throughout the province to administer government regulations in eight separate regions.

To assist anglers in understanding the current regulations the BC government distributes a synopsis, *Freshwater Fishing*, through most marinas and locations where licences may be purchased. This 72-page summary is strictly a guideline to sports fishers and should not be interpreted as replacing the Fisheries Act of Canada.

The guides explains BC's fish tagging program as well as gear and boating restrictions.

British Columbia also has an extensive catch and release program. In some cases certain species **must** be released; in others anglers can pay a conservation surcharge to retain their catch.

Licences are required by both BC residents and non-residents.

If asked, you must allow a Park Ranger or an RCMP, Conservation or Fisheries Officer to examine your catch and fishing gear.

If you employ a guide ask to see their licence as it is illegal to guide for compensation without such a licence.

Fish and Wildlife Regional Offices

Vancouver Island: 2080A Labieux Road, Nanaimo, BC V9T 6J9
(250) 751-3100

Lower Mainland: 10470 - 152 St., Surrey, BC V3R 0Y3
(604) 582-5200 or 1-800-665-7027 (toll free)

Thompson-Nicola: 1259 Dalhousie Dr., Kamloops, BC V2C 5Z5
(250) 371-6200

Kootenay: 401-333 Victoria St., Nelson, BC V1L 4K3
(250)354-6333

or

205 Industrial Rd. G, Cranbrook, BC V1C 6H3
(250) 489-8540

Cariboo: Ste 400, 640 Borland St, Williams Lake, BC V2G 4T1
(250)398-4530

Skeena: 3726 Alfred St., Smithers, BC V0J 2N0
(250) 847-7303

Omineca: 1011-4th Ave, Prince George, BC V2L3H9
(250) 565-6135

Peace: 10003-110th Ave., Fort St. John, BC V1J 6M7
(250) 787-3411

Okanagan: 201, 3547 Skaha Lk Rd., Penticton, BC V2A 7K2
(250) 490-8200

The Author

Jack is a long-time resident of Kamloops, B.C. Recently named as an honorary member of the B.C. Fly Fishing Museum, Jack Shaw is truly part of our fly-fishing heritage.

After seven decades of avid sports fishing and the methodical development of new fly designs, Jack has become one of the most respected anglers in central B.C. Much of the popularity of fly fishing in the Kamloops area is attributable to Jack Shaw's writings over the years.

"I feel like he mentored me in print," Gary Stephens, vice chairman of the B.C. Federation of Fly Fishers, recently stated.

> *Jack Shaw, in my opinion, knows more about how to fly fish successfully in trout lakes than anyone else in the world. He can come away regularly with a string when everyone else on the lake has been skunked.*
>
> Mike Cramond